The Norman Conquests

THE NORMAN CONQUESTS

TABLE MANNERS
LIVING TOGETHER
ROUND AND ROUND THE GARDEN

ALAN AYCKBOURN

SAMUEL   FRENCH

LONDON
NEW YORK   TORONTO   SYDNEY   HOLLYWOOD

ISBN 0 573 01576 7

THE NORMAN CONQUESTS

TABLE MANNERS

A play

ALAN AYCKBOURN

SAMUEL FRENCH

LONDON
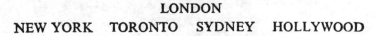
NEW YORK   TORONTO   SYDNEY   HOLLYWOOD

ISBN 0 573 01575 9

TABLE MANNERS

First presented by the Library Theatre Co., Scarborough in June 1973 and subsequently by the Greenwich Theatre Company in May 1974, and in London by Michael Codron at the Globe Theatre in August 1974, with the following cast of characters:

Norman	Tom Courtenay
Tom	Michael Gambon
Sarah	Penelope Keith
Annie	Felicity Kendal
Reg	Mark Kingston
Ruth	Bridget Turner

The play directed by Eric Thompson
Setting by Alan Pickford

The action passes in the dining-room of a Victorian vicarage-type house during a week-end in July

ACT I
    Scene 1   Saturday, 6 p.m.
    Scene 2   Sunday, 9 a.m.

ACT II
    Scene 1   Sunday, 8 p.m.
    Scene 2   Monday, 8 a.m.

Period – the present

ACT I

Scene 1

The dining-room. Saturday, 6 p.m.

It is a fine evening, the sun streams through the french windows of the room. There are four chairs with a solid table, a sideboard, two window-seats and a couple of easy chairs. The room is large and high-ceilinged, and like the rest of this Victorian vicarage-type building, badly needs redecorating

As the Curtain *rises, Annie in a baggy cardigan, jeans and raffia slippers, enters with a flower vase of water. She thumps this down in the middle of the table, picks up the roses which lie beside it and drops them into the vase. She gives the whole lot a final shake and that, as far as she is concerned, concludes her flower arrangement*

Sarah (*off*) Hallo! Hallo, we're here!

Sarah enters. She wears a light summer coat and dress. She is breathless

Annie Sarah!

Sarah (*embracing her*) Annie dear . . .

Annie Good journey?

Sarah Oh, yes, yes, not too bad. Reg drove far too fast as usual but we got here—oh, it's lovely to come down. I've been looking forward to this week-end away from it all for weeks. Week-end? It's barely a day. You've no idea how that dreary little house of ours gets me down.

Annie Oh, it's not bad.

Sarah Try living there sometime. Not a decent shop, not a cinema, not even a hairdresser—except some awful place I can't go into because of the smell. I said to Reg, for goodness' sake you're an estate agent, surely you can get the pick of anywhere and then we finish up in somewhere like that. You're so lucky, Annie, you have no idea. Just to see a tree once in a while and the birds—I really miss it. Now then, how are you, let's look. Oh, Annie darling, you look just the same. Your hair . . .

Annie (*self-consciously smoothing her tangle*) I know—I haven't brushed it today. I washed it, though, this morning.

Sarah What's the good of washing it if you don't brush it. It's like a gorse bush.

Annie Well, nobody sees it. The postman, the milkman, couple of cows and Mother.

Sarah And Tom.

Annie Oh, yes. Tom.

Sarah You mustn't forget Tom. And how's Mother?

Annie No better, no worse. She hasn't felt like getting up, not for weeks . . .

Sarah Well, you should make her. She needs to.

Annie Old Wickham says if she doesn't want to, don't make her.

Sarah Wickham? Oh, yes, I've never really cared for him. His eyes are too close together. Still, I suppose he's all right as a doctor. He must be better than ours. I mean, this business with my back was practically criminal.

Annie Your back?

Sarah Surely I wrote and told you? I'm sure I did. I was so upset I wrote to everybody.

Annie Oh, yes.

Sarah Annie, I must buy you a new jumper, remind me.

Annie I'm attached to this one.

Sarah I should think you are—you were wearing it at Christmas. We'll have to chisel it off you . . . Mmm, lovely flowers. Now tell me. Where are you going?

Annie When?

Sarah For your week-end, where are you going?

Annie Well . . .

Sarah Oh, come on. Don't be so secretive.

Annie Well—I was going to Hastings.

Sarah Oh, lovely! Hastings is gorgeous. I think I was there with Reg just before we were married. There's a heavenly little pub somewhere . . .

Annie No, well I couldn't get in at Hastings.

Sarah Couldn't get in?

Annie No, it was all booked. I forgot it was summer.

Sarah Oh. Yes. Well, where are you going?

Annie I rather fancied East Grinstead.

Sarah East Grinstead?

Annie Yes.

Sarah What an extraordinary idea. What on earth made you choose there?

Annie Well, it sounded—interesting.

Sarah Yes, I suppose it is. I've never heard of anybody having a holiday in East Grinstead. I suppose they do—but I've never heard of anybody.

Annie Well, I am.

Sarah Yes. I think I'd have almost preferred Eastbourne but . . . (*Displaying her outfit*) Do you like this?

Annie Super.

Sarah (*taking off her coat, touching the back of the chair for dust, then putting the coat over it*) It was like a tent on me when I bought it, but I had it altered. I'm rather pleased. Now, you're to leave everything to me. I'm taking over. Just tell me what pills and potions Mother has and when she has them and then off you go.

Annie I've written it down somewhere. I'll show you. The only difficult things are her drops.

Sarah Oh well, if they're difficult Reg can cope witn them. He's going to do most of the running up and down stairs anyway. I mean, this is a a holiday for me, too. She's his mother. He can do something for her for a change.

Annie How is he?

Sarah Reg? (*With a big sigh*) Oh well, he's still Reg you know. I've tried God knows I've tried, but he'll always be basically Reg. You'll know, he's your brother after all. There are times when I think he's sleep-walking. I have to force him to make an effort. Heaven knows how he runs a business. I'd certainly never let him sell a house of mine.

Annie I've left you a cold supper.

Sarah Oh, you shouldn't have bothered.

Annie Well, I knew you wouldn't want to be . . .

Sarah You shouldn't have bothered.

Annie I left it all out for you on the——

Sarah You really shouldn't have bothered.

Annie —kitchen table.

Sarah Lovely.

Annie I was just laying things in here.

Sarah Oh, there's no need for that. We'll eat with our fingers. We're on holiday, for heaven's sake.

Annie We do have knives and forks. (*She takes two sets of knives, forks and spoons from the sideboard to the table*

Sarah I'll find them, don't bother. Now please, just get changed and go.

Annie Okay. (*She starts to move to the door*)

Sarah Oh. I nearly forgot. How's Tom?

Annie Tom? Oh, fine. I think.

Sarah Still seeing a lot of him?

Annie Oh, yes. He's generally around. When he's not out curing his sick animals. He's here at the moment, actually. The cat's got something wrong with its paw.

Sarah (*arranging the flowers*) It must be fascinating being a vet. It's a pity in a way he's not a proper doctor.

Annie He is a proper doctor. He just prefers animals to people.

Sarah That came from the heart.

Annie No. He just likes animals. Don't think he's very fond of our cat, but he likes most animals.

Sarah Yes, he's a bit—heavy going, isn't he? I've always found him a trifle ponderous. Perhaps it's shyness.

Annie No, I think he's probably ponderous.

Sarah So he hasn't—er—shown any more interest?

Annie In what?

Sarah Well, you. At Christmas, we thought he was beginning to sit up and take notice of you just a little. Pricking up his ears.

Annie Like a mongrel with a pedigree bitch.

Sarah Yes, well . . .

Annie Honestly, stop trying to pair us off. He just comes round when he's bored, that's all.

Sarah A man doesn't spend as much time as Tom does round here without having a very good reason. Believe you me. You don't have to be psychic to know what that is.

Annie Well, if it's that he's never asked for it and even if he did he wouldn't get it. So I don't know why he bothers. (*She sets out the knives and forks*)

Sarah Annie! You're getting dreadfully coarse.

Annie Oh, you're just a prude. (*She takes out two side plates, two napkins and two rush mats, and sets them on the table*)

Sarah No, I'm not a prude. No, I've never been called that. You can't call me a prude. That's not fair, Annie. I mean, I don't care for smutty talk or dirty jokes. I just don't find them funny. Or particularly tasteful. But that isn't being a prude. That's normal decent behaviour which is something quite different.

Annie Yes.

Sarah I won't have the television set on at all, these days.

Annie Anyway, all that happens is that Tom comes round here like he has done for years. I feed him. He sits and broods. Sometimes we talk. That's all.

Sarah Talk about what?

Annie (*disarranging the flowers as she moves around the table*) Oh, super exciting things like does the kitchen ceiling need another coat and distemper and hardpad and foot and mouth and swine vesicular disease. Then I pot Mother and retire to bed—alone—itching.

Sarah Oh.

Annie And count diseased sheep crashing headlong into the gate. Look for all I know he may be passionately in love with me. He may be flashing out all sorts of secret signals which I just haven't noticed. But he's never even put a hand on my knee. (*Reflecting*) God forbid.

Sarah But you're fond of him?

Annie He's—very kind. Yes, I like him a lot. I sometimes miss him when he's not here. I suppose that means something.

Sarah Yes. You see, I was rather hoping—I know it's wicked of me—I was rather hoping that you were both planning to go off for this weekend together.

Annie Oh. No.

Sarah You're not, are you?

Annie (*uneasily*) No. Not at all.

Sarah Are you sure?

Annie Of course I'm sure.

Sarah You're looking very shifty.

Annie I'm not. Honestly. No. Stop it.

Sarah Stop what?

Annie Looking at me like that.

Sarah Like what?

Annie Like that. Stop it.

Sarah You're a dreadful liar.

Annie I'm not.

Sarah Listen, if you are, there's no need to keep it a secret from me. I mean, you said I'm a prude but I've just proved I'm not, surely? I mentioned it first. I think it's splendid. I think if you and Tom were to get away from this house, away from Mother and everything—it's the best thing you could do. It's what you both need. (*She kisses her*) Very sensible.

Annie Yes.

Sarah Have a lovely time. I only wish it were me. Not with Tom, of course. But I think that's what we all need now and then, don't we? A nice dirty week-end somewhere. Oh, it's so exciting. I am pleased you're doing it. I think the best bit is waking up in the morning in a strange room and finding some exciting-looking man beside you and— you've got a double room?

Annie It's a bit more complicated than that.

Sarah Oh? How do you mean? You haven't got a double room?

Annie No, it's just . . .

Sarah What? You're not pregnant?

Annie No.

Sarah Oh, thank God.

Annie No, it's just—oh golly, I didn't mean to tell you.

Sarah Tell me what?

Annie It's awfully sordid. You're sure you want to hear?

Sarah Of course, I want to hear.

Annie It'll shock you.

Sarah My dear, I've been married for eight years. I've had two children. I think I've just about seen everything there is to see. I defy you to shock me. I honestly defy you.

Annie Well. Last Christmas, when you were all here . . .

Sarah Yes?

Annie You and Reg and Ruth and Norman. And then you and Reg left early . . .

Sarah Because Denise didn't want to miss her dancing classes—yes?

Annie And then after that, Ruth was ill . . .

Sarah Or so she said.

Annie Well, she was flat on her back with something for a week and that left Norman and me—more or less to cope. Tom was in Scotland on a course.

Sarah Yes?

Annie Anyway.

Sarah I'm beginning dreadfully not to like the sound of this one little bit.

Annie Anyway. Golly, I'm getting dreadfully hot.

Sarah Go on. What?

Annie Well, you know Norman, he's . . .

Sarah Yes, I know Norman very well.

Annie He's not a bit like Tom. I mean, just the opposite to Tom. Norman doesn't bother with secret signals at all. It was just wham, thump and there we both were on the rug.

Sarah Rug?

Annie Yes.
Sarah Which rug?
Annie The brown nylon fur one in the lounge . . . (*She starts to giggle*)
Sarah (*irritated*) What is it? Why are you laughing?
Annie (*unable to control herself*) Does it matter which rug?
Sarah I don't think it's funny.
Annie No, nor do I. I'm sorry—it's just I'm so embarrassed—oh, gosh . . .
Sarah Annie, pull yourself together.
Annie (*helplessly*) Yes . . .
Sarah (*thumping the table*) Annie, what happened on the rug?
Annie Everything happened on the rug.
Sarah Does Ruth know?
Annie No.
Sarah Or Tom?
Annie No. (*Drying her eyes*) Oh, dear . . .
Sarah Well, I blame Norman. That is absolutely typical—fur rug!

This starts Annie off again

> It's just the sort of thing . . . Annie, will you stop making that ridiculous
> noise—typical behaviour.

Annie blows her nose

> Is that it? Was that the only occasion?

Annie Oh, yes. Ruth got better and they both went home.
Sarah I suppose it could have been worse. That poor woman. I mean, I
don't have a lot of time for Ruth, as you know. Personally, I find her
snide little remarks, her violent ups and downs just too much to cope
with. I know she's your sister, I'm sorry for talking like this. However,
I would not wish my worst enemy married to a man like—not even
Ruth. Heaven knows why they married. Never understood it. What did
she see in him?
Annie Norman says it was uncontrollable animal lust that drew them
together.
Sarah Norman told you that?
Annie Yes. He says it's died out now. They are like two empty husks.
Sarah Yes. Hardly surprising. Well, believe me, you're well clear of that,
dear. You're well clear of that one.
Annie You don't think I should then?
Sarah What?
Annie Go.
Sarah Go where?
Annie This week-end.
Sarah This week-end?
Annie With Norman. To East Grinstead.

A pause

Sarah You were planning to go with Norman to East Grinstead?

Annie Yes. He couldn't get in anywhere else.

Sarah You're not serious?

Annie Yes.

Sarah But how could you even think of it?

Annie He asked me.

Sarah What has that to do with it?

Annie Well, I wanted a holiday . . .

Sarah Yes, but—this wouldn't be just a holiday. I mean, I mean, you just don't go off on holiday with your sister's husband.

Annie It was only a week-end. I needed a holiday.

Sarah Well, you could have gone on your own.

Annie (*slightly angry*) I didn't want to go on my own. I'm always on my own.

Sarah But did you realize what you would be getting yourself into?

Annie Well—the way Norman put it—it sounded simple. Just a week-end.

Sarah Norman will put it any way which suits Norman. Did you think of Ruth? And Tom?

Annie Oh, to hell with Tom. He could have asked me if he'd wanted to, but he didn't. If I wait to be asked by Tom, I won't even get on an old folks' outing,

Sarah Well, what about Ruth?

Annie That's up to Norman. He wrote to me and then he phoned and asked me and I suddenly thought, well yes—I think, actually if I'm being really truthful and, knowing Norman, I didn't think it would ever happen.

Sarah You were certain enough about it to get Reg and I down. We've had all the trouble of having to take the children to their grandparents so that we wouldn't have to bring them down here because we knew they would disturb Mother. I've had all the trouble of delegating responsibility for the Bring and Buy Sale which I'm sure will be a disaster because I'm the only one among them with any sort of organizing ability. And Reg has had to cancel his golf.

Annie I'm sorry. I've been feeling sick all morning. I'm sorry.

Sarah Yes, well I'm sure we all are.

Annie Well . . . (*She moves to the door*)

Sarah Where are you going?

Annie I don't know. I was just—I don't know.

Sarah I think it's just as well we are here. You quite obviously need a rest. Now, I want you to sit down here and leave everything to me.

Annie No, it's all right, I . . .

Sarah And let's get this quite clear to start with. You are not going anywhere. Not while I'm in this house.

Annie What about my week-end?

Sarah You can have your week-end here. Reg and I will cope. That's what we came down for. You can rest. You can certainly forget the idea of going anywhere with Norman. That's final. You're staying here.

Annie Yes. I rather thought I would be.

Sarah What you need is rest.

Tom enters from the garden

Tom Ah.

Sarah Tom! How nice to see you, Tom. (*She shakes Tom's hand*)

Tom Hallo, Sarah. Keeping fit?

Sarah Tom, I've just been saying I think Annie's honestly been overdoing it.

Tom Really? Do you think so?

Sarah You really must take more care of her, Tom. We all expect you to keep an eye on her, you know, when we're not here.

Tom Do my best.

Sarah She's rather your responsibility.

Tom Yes, can't have that. Been trying to get that cat out of the tree. Your cat's gone up a tree, Annie.

Annie Oh.

Sarah Anyway, Annie's just decided she's not going away this week-end. She's going to stay here and have a good rest.

Tom Septic paw, you know.

Sarah And Reg and I will be here to look after her.

Tom That's good news. Aren't you going then?

Annie No.

Sarah With your help, of course, Tom. You must stay for supper.

Tom Supper?

Sarah Mustn't he, Annie?

Annie Why not.

Tom Save me opening a tin at home.

Sarah Lovely. Now, I must just pop up and see Mother. Then I'll come down and organize everything. Leave it all to Reg and me. Where is Reg? I asked him to bring the cases in ages ago.

Tom I left him in the garden.

Sarah What's he doing in the garden?

Tom Nothing much. Just talking to Norman.

Sarah Norman? Norman is here?

Tom Yes.

Sarah Norman is here, under this roof?

Tom No, he's in the garden. We were chatting away.

Sarah Oh, my God. Chatting about what?

Tom Various subjects. Cats. And his pyjamas.

Sarah Pyjamas?

Tom Yes, he was showing them to me.

Sarah Do you mean he's wearing them?

Tom No. He was just generally waving them about.

Sarah Tom, stay here with Annie. Don't move. Stay here. I'll be back.

Sarah hurries out to the garden

Tom Did you know Norman was here?

Annie Yes. I saw him earlier.

Tom Oh. Were you expecting him?

Annie Not really, no.

Tom Ah. Well. (*He stares out of the window*)

Annie (*in frustration*) Oh.

Tom Put your feet up.

Annie What?

Tom I should put your feet up.

Annie (*rising and going to the sideboard*) No. Not at the moment. (*She gets out the cruet, two more mats, knives, forks and spoons, and a biscuit tin*)

Tom I'm a bit worried about that paw, you know.

Annie Paw?

Tom On the cat. Needs looking at. (*Moving in Annie's way*) Does he have a name, by the way?

Annie What? No. Just cat. (*She moves round Tom to the table and lays it*)

Tom That's all right, I don't suppose he minds. Preferable to Oscar or Herbert or something. He probably wouldn't answer to it if he had one. Cats' names are more for human benefit. They give one a certain degree more confidence that the animal belongs to you. Of course, they never do. Cats belong to no-one but themselves.

Annie Oh, I'm so stupid . . . (*She bangs down the cutlery*)

Tom All right?

Annie Yes. I just feel such a fool.

Tom Oh. Not much answer to that, is there. (*Picking up the biscuit tin*) Mind if I have a water biscuit?

Annie Have the lot.

Tom No. Just one. It'll spoil my dinner. Ah, high baked . . .

Annie Tom . . .

Tom (*crunching*) Um?

Annie What did you think when I said I was going away this week-end?

Tom Well, I don't know. I suppose I thought—you were going away this week-end. (*Holding out the tin*) Want one?

Annie (*irritated*) No . . .

Tom They're a bit stale. No, it did occur to me you might have liked someone to come along with you . . .

Annie It did?

Tom And then I thought, well, probably not.

Annie Why? What on earth made you think I wanted to go off and sit in some dreary hotel room on my own?

Tom Yes, it did seem rather odd, I must say.

Annie How long have you known me?

Tom Oh—years . . .

Annie Years. And in all that time have I ever even hinted that I'd like to go off on my own?

Tom Not as far as I know.

Annie (*angrily*) Then why the hell should I suddenly decide to do it now?

Tom Well, I don't know. Simmer down.

Annie Why didn't you say—Annie, will you be all right on your own?

Would you like company? Someone to come along, too? Someone to
talk to? Why didn't you think of saying it? Just once.
Tom Oh, come on . . .
Annie Or was the whole prospect just too awful?
Tom No . . .
Annie Well, then?
Tom You should have said something. You should have asked me along.
I'd've come. You should've asked me.
Annie (*weakly*) Oh, dear God. Yes, I'd have had to have done.
Tom Don't blame me.
Annie I'm not blaming you. Oh—nun's knickers!
Tom Language. You're getting awfully het up. I should put your feet up.
Annie I don't want to put my bloody feet up.

Annie stamps out

*Tom gazes after her, slightly puzzled. He helps himself to another biscuit,
then puts the tin on the table. Reg is heard calling from the garden*

Reg (*off*) Annie, Annie, Annie!

Reg bursts in from the garden

Where is she then? Where's that little sister of mine. (*Seeing no-one but
Tom*) Oh. Where is she?
Tom No idea. Kitchen, possibly.
Reg Ah. He's a laugh, you know.
Tom Who?
Reg Norman. Goes on and on. Don't know what he's talking about.
Makes me laugh, though. I don't care, I like him. She doesn't but I do.
Women don't, you know. Not many women like him. Don't know why.
Sarah can't bear him. Won't have him in the house. Nor will his wife.
(*He laughs*)
Tom I think Annie gets on all right with him.
Reg Ah well. Annie. (*He smiles affectionately*) She's something special.
You'll be all right with her, Tom. Take my word. If you decide to marry
any of us, marry her. Not that I'm saying you should but if you did.
Mind you, you can't marry Ruth and I don't think you'd fancy me, so
there's not much choice, is there? (*He laughs*)
Tom Um. (*Thoughtfully*) They're all a bit peculiar at the moment.
Reg Who are?
Tom The women. All on edge, for some reason.
Reg The women are restless tonight, eh? Full moon.
Tom Eh?
Reg Probably a full moon. (*He bays like a hound and laughs*)
Tom No. Something startled them.
Reg Norman. Or mice. One or the other. I hear Annie's not going now.
Tom Apparently not.

Reg Could have had my golf. If I'd known. Never mind. Better go and see Mother in a minute. Sarah's up there at the moment. I'll wait till she comes down. Two of them, too much of a good thing. I'll put it off as long as I can. Mother always says the same thing. What did you go and marry her for? Biggest mistake of your life. You'll live to regret it. Trouble is, I can never think of a convincing answer. (*He laughs*) She's probably right. I mean, there are compensations. Children—sometimes. Even Sarah—sometimes. But when I sit here in this house and listen to the quiet. You know, I wonder why I left. I had my own room here, you know. All my books, my own desk, a shelf for my hobbies. I'd sit up there in my school holidays—happy as a sandboy. I'd make these balsa wood aeroplanes. Dozens of them. Very satisfying. Mind you, they never flew. Soon as I launched them—crack—nose dive—firewood. But it didn't really matter. It was a hell of a bore winding them up, anyway. I built one for the kids the other day. They didn't really take to it. Where's the guns, Dad? Where are the bombs then? (*He shakes his head*) Oh well, what do you expect.

Tom No, you see—I think I've stopped her from going.

Reg Who?

Tom Annie.

Reg You have?

Tom Yes . . .

Reg Hope we'll get some dinner soon. I'm getting peckish. (*He takes a biscuit from the tin, leaving the lid off*)

Tom You see, she didn't want to go on her own.

Reg On holiday? Ah well. Who does?

Tom She was rather expecting me to offer to come, too.

Reg Oh. You should have been in there—like a shot, eh?

Tom Yes.

Reg While you had the chance. These are stale.

Tom Now, I've gone and upset her.

Reg Oh, dear.

Tom I've never been very good at that sort of thing. Always seem to miss the moment.

Reg That's how it goes, isn't it?

Tom Yes. I've let her down. I can feel myself doing it while I'm doing it. I suppose I'll have to find a way of making it up.

Reg I shouldn't bother. It'll blow over. Wait for the new moon.

Sarah enters from the house

Tom picks up some cutlery from the table

Sarah What are you doing in here?

Reg Oh. I beg your pardon. Is the dining-room closed? (*He laughs to Tom*)

Sarah Where's Annie?

Reg Getting us something to eat, I hope. Slaving over a hot stove.

Sarah She is not. Anyway, it's a cold meal. Where is she?

Reg I don't know.

Sarah You haven't left her in the living-room with Norman.

Reg Possibly. What's wrong? He's all right, he won't bite her.

Sarah Oh, my God.

Reg Tom'll inject her for rabies, won't you, Tom?

Tom I'll go and look for her if you . . .

Reg Inject her for rabies.

Sarah No, Tom, stay where you are. Reg.

Reg What?

Sarah Go and see if they're in there.

Reg Why don't you?

Sarah Because I'd rather you did, please.

Reg I'm not interested if they're in there. It doesn't matter to me if they're in there or not. You're the one who's interested if they're in there.

Sarah (*sharply*) Will you please do as I ask for once. Besides it'll look much more natural.

Tom I say, what's going on?

Sarah (*soothingly*) Nothing to worry about, Tom, nothing at all.

Reg I don't think it'll look more natural. I mean, what's natural about me walking in there, having a look and then walking out again.

Sarah Well, pretend you've gone to fetch something. Use your imagination, for heaven's sake.

Reg All right. All right. What am I supposed to be fetching?

Sarah I don't know. Anything.

Reg (*moving to the door and then pausing*) What's all this about a cold meal? What sort of cold meal?

Sarah Cold meat and salad. Now, go on.

Reg If there's one thing I can't stand when I'm hungry it's salad.

Reg goes out to the house

Sarah He's a difficult man. (*She takes the cutlery from Tom and replaces it*) He is such a difficult man. Ask him to do a simple thing for you and there's a twenty-minute argument. Did you talk to Annie? (*She rearranges the flowers*)

Tom Yes.

Sarah Did she—say anything?

Tom She—told me the reason why she'd planned the whole week-end. Why it had fallen through.

Sarah Oh. (*She pats his hand*)

Tom I could kick myself for being so slow off the mark.

Sarah You mustn't blame yourself.

Tom I'm afraid I do, rather.

Sarah I don't see why. I mean, you weren't to know that . . .

Reg enters with a waste-paper basket

Reg Yes, they're in there.
Sarah What's that?

Tom takes a fork from the table and wanders to the window

Reg Waste-paper basket, isn't it?
Sarah Couldn't you have found something a little more natural?
Reg What did you expect me to bring back? A bloody grand piano? (*He sits in the easy chair with the basket on his knee*)
Sarah Right, Tom.
Tom Um?
Sarah I think it's high time you went in and said your piece.
Tom Really?
Sarah Told them where you stand.
Tom Me?
Sarah Make sure Norman knows.
Tom Norman?
Sarah You'll lose your chance if you don't do it soon.
Tom (*baffled*) Oh, yes.

Reg bays like a hound

Sarah What are you doing?
Reg Nothing. Full moon, that's all. Full moon. (*He nods and winks at Tom*)
Tom Ah.

Sarah takes the fork from Tom and pushes him out

Tom goes out bewildered

Reg drums on the basket

Sarah I think this may have worked out for the best. Might even stir Tom into action, you never know. You haven't been eating these biscuits?
Reg I squelched through a couple.
Sarah You'll spoil your meal.
Reg Oh yes. All that lovely lettuce.
Sarah You and your stomach. I'd rather hoped I was in for a quiet weekend for once. It seems it's not to be. Look at these forks, they haven't been cleaned since we were last here. It's a crying shame. All this silver. (*She takes a duster from the sideboard and vigorously polishes the cutlery*)
Reg Are we staying or going?
Sarah We can hardly go home.
Reg I thought the whole point of our being here was to look after Mother but if Annie's going to be here . . .
Sarah I don't know about being here to look after Mother. We need someone here to look after her.
Reg She's managed up till now. There's Tom.
Sarah Oh, Tom. There's no point in relying on him. I mean, he's pleasant

enough, but I don't think he's quite all there. That's a terrible thing to say, but look at the way he's behaved. Mind you, she does precious little to encourage him. How is she going to attract any man looking like that, let alone Tom.

Reg She's all right. Leave her alone.

Sarah Do you realize what would happen if I did?

Reg She can manage.

Sarah I take it you've gathered what's going on in this house?

Reg What?

Sarah Where have you been for the last hour?

Reg What do you mean, where have I been? You know where I've been. I've been here, waiting for something to eat.

Sarah Norman had planned to take Annie away to a hotel this week-end.

Reg Norman?

Sarah Yes.

Reg With Annie?

Sarah Yes.

Reg Was she the one he was taking to East Grinstead?

Sarah (*impatiently*) Of course she was.

Reg gives a yell of delight

(*When this has died down, coolly*) Frankly, Reg, I think there's something mentally wrong with you. I think you ought to see someone. I'm being serious. How you can take so little interest in your own family, your own sister.

Reg Oh, Sarah, come on. (*He puts the waste-paper basket down and rises*) Sit down. You've done nothing but run round and round. I think it's funny, I can't help it.

Sarah You're the same at home. Exactly the same.

Reg Oh, now, come on . . . (*He moves away*)

Sarah Yes, you can walk away but it's always left for me to deal with, isn't it? It's left for me to apologize to people for you. It's left to me to explain why you walk straight upstairs as soon as anyone comes to visit us.

Reg They're your friends.

Sarah It's me that's left looking stupid in front of the headmistress when you forget the names of our own children . . .

Reg That was only once.

Sarah They run wild those children. You've done nothing for them. Nothing at all. If I didn't get them food, they'd starve, if I didn't buy them clothes, they'd be naked—you sit in that room, which I spend my whole life trying to keep tidy, fiddling with aeroplanes and bits of cardboard and now you can't even be bothered with your own sister . . .

Reg Sarah, please, would you kindly stop talking.

Sarah No, I will not stop talking.

Reg You have talked at me since I got up this morning—you have talked at me over breakfast . . .

Sarah It happens to be the only way I can get through to you . . .

Reg You talked solidly in the car for an hour—nearly causing us to have a very serious accident . . .
Sarah Which was entirely your fault.
Reg And ever since we've been here, you haven't stopped for a second. Now, for the love of God, shut up.

A slight pause

Sarah (*stopping polishing and sitting at the table*) I will not be spoken to like that. (*Tearful now*) I will not have you raising your voice to me like that. Just who do you think it is you're talking to?
Reg I think, like you, I'm talking to a brick wall. I'm going for a walk.
Sarah (*hysterically*) All right, go. Go on then. Go, you beastly little man.

Sarah snatches up the biscuit tin from the table and hurls it at Reg. It hits the sideboard, biscuits fly in all directions

Reg Sarah!

Sarah sits sobbing. Reg stands uselessly

   Annie comes in from the house

Annie Oh.

Reg starts to pick up the biscuits

Reg Biscuits.
Annie (*moving to him*) Oh, yes. (*Helping Reg*) Here, let me . . . (*Mouthing to Reg*) What's the matter?
Reg (*mouthing*) Nothing.
Annie (*pointing at Sarah, mouthing*) Is she all right?

Reg shrugs

   (*Looking at Sarah and shrugging*) I'll get the dustpan.

   Annie goes out

Sarah You're contemptible.
Reg (*kneeling down to collect biscuits and tin*) You really must control that temper of yours, you know.

   Tom enters from the house. He pauses as he takes in the scene

Reg, crawling on the floor, does not see him. Nor does Sarah, with her back to him

Sarah You are the most contemptible man I've ever known.
Reg The feeling's mutual, don't worry.

   Tom goes out to the house, looking worried

Sarah God knows what's going to happen to us. God knows.

Annie returns with the dustpan

Annie Here we are. Soon clear this up.
Reg Sorry about this.
Annie Oh well. Accidents happen, don't they.
Sarah It wasn't an accident.
Annie Oh.
Reg No. The biscuits were so stale they threw themselves off the table in desperation.
Sarah What have you decided, Annie?
Annie What? Oh well—it's all rather settled itself, hasn't it? I'm staying here, of course. (*She stands up*)
Sarah I mean, it's entirely up to you. I mean, all I was doing was trying to . . .
Annie Well, it's probably best.

Reg wanders away to the window

Sarah Tom and Norman have sorted out their differences, have they?
Annie I don't think there were any, really. Norman's getting drunk and Tom's looking thoughtful
Sarah Oh well, I've done what I can. I'm sorry, I think the man must be mentally defective. I think they both are. I'll bring some things in.
Annie It's all right, I'll . . .
Sarah No—no—no! I want to. (*Collecting her coat*) I want to bring some things in.

Sarah goes out to the house

Reg We seem to have upset your week-end. (*He sits by the table*)
Annie (*putting the dustpan by the sideboard*) Not really. It was a mad idea. (*Moving to the table, disarranging the flowers*) Rather flattering all the same. Suddenly having two men bidding for my favours. Even if they are Tom and Norman.
Reg (*chuckling*) Well, I must say—didn't know I had a sister like you. (*He pulls Annie on to his knee*)
Annie (*amused*) It's ridiculous, really.
Reg I knew one of us took after Mother—I couldn't think who it was. Certainly it wasn't me or Ruth.
Annie Not Ruth.
Reg Do you remember Mother taking us on holiday? Where was it? Weston-super-Mare. Were you old enough to remember?
Annie You mean when she picked up that sailor?
Reg Yes. He kept throwing that ball half a mile down the beach. Trying to get us all to run after it. Run along, kids. Go and fetch it. Let me talk to your mum.
Annie And Ruth wouldn't go.

Reg No, she wouldn't budge.

Annie "I'm staying here to look after Mother. I don't trust him . . ." There was Mother saying, "Run along, Ruth dear. Run along and play . . ."

Reg Then there was that Polish rear gunner.

Annie Oh God, yes. And Father suddenly came home on leave.

Reg That drain-pipe's still broken, you know. I had a look.

Annie and Reg laugh

Sarah enters with a jar of salad cream. She bangs it on the table and glares at them

Annie and Reg are silent

Sarah (*icily*) Don't let me spoil the joke. (*She takes the flowers to the sideboard and rearranges them*) I'm sure you both find me terribly amusing. I'm sure you all find me hilarious.

Annie Not at all.

Tom comes on laughing heartily, carrying a bottle

Sarah wheels on him and glares. Tom stops laughing

Sarah goes out to the house

Sarah . . .

Annie goes out after Sarah

Reg What was the joke?

Tom Nothing really. Norman told me to come in and try to jolly things up. Doesn't seem to have worked.

Reg Hardly at all.

Norman is heard singing briefly from the sitting-room—"Girls were made to Love and Kiss". Reg and Tom register

Tom Norman! (*Holding up the bottle*) I brought a bottle of this. Help wash down the radishes. Managed to salvage it. Norman's drunk most of them. (*He puts it on the table*)

Reg I didn't know we had anything like that in this house.

Tom (*getting two glasses from the sideboard*) Home-made. Mother made it last year. Just before she was ill. Annie and I bottled it. Tastes revolting but it's very potent.

Reg Carrot. Does it have to be carrot?

Tom (*opening the bottle and pouring*) Well, there's also parsnip or dandelion, but this seems to have a slightly better bouquet. The dandelion's all right but I lost the use of one side of my face for about an hour after I drunk it. (*Handing a glass to Reg*) Here, what do you think?

Reg (*tasting it*) Not bad. Not bad at all. (*Rising as it hits his stomach*)
Oh, good grief.
Tom I think it's an acquired taste.
Reg You must have a stomach like a blast furnace.
Norman (*off, singing*) "Am I to blame if God has made me gay?"

Annie enters with a tray of four plates of salad which she puts on the side-board. Sarah follows and sits at the table

Annie Grub's up. (*She puts two plates on the table*)
Reg Ah-ha, the great caterpillar hunt is on.
Annie (*bringing two glasses to the table*) No, it isn't, I washed the lettuce
this time.
Reg (*moving to the table*) Oh, yes.
Annie (*bringing the remaining two plates to the table*) Well, I rinsed it under
the tap. Twice. (*She sits at the table*)
Tom Shall I give Norman a call?
Sarah No.
Reg What I always say about your salads, Annie, is that I may not enjoy
eating them but I learn an arful lot about insect biology. My appreciation
of the anatomy of an earwig has increased enormously . . . (*He sits*)
Sarah Could we keep off this subject, please.
Tom Wine, Sarah?
Sarah What is it?
Tom Wine. Home-made.
Sarah Oh well, just a little.

Tom pours wine for Sarah, then for all the others

Thank you.

Tom sits and tucks his napkin under his chin. They all eat in silence

Reg Could you pass the centipede sauce, please.

Annie giggles. Sarah glares

(*Raising his glass*) Well, here's to us . . .
Sarah I think it would be fitting to drink to Annie and Tom.
Tom Really? Why is that?
Annie Because we're here.
Tom Oh, I see. I thought there was a special reason.
Sarah That's rather up to you, isn't it, Tom?
Tom Um?
Reg Cheers, anyway.
Sarah Good health, Tom, Annie.
Reg Tom and Annie.
Tom Tom and Annie.
Sarah Oh! It's really rather . . .

*Sarah drinks, puts down her glass. Her stomach explodes. She lets out a
gasp. Tom and Annie half rise*

Annie Sarah!
Tom All right? (*He begins to bang her back rather heartily*)
Sarah (*regaining her breath*) Yes—it took me by surprise.
Annie Yes, it tends to do that.
Sarah (*not enjoying Tom's attentions*) That will do, Tom, thank you. That
will do.
Reg It'll kill off any beetles you've swallowed.
Sarah Will you stop making remarks like that.
Reg (*raising his knife by way of apology*) Sorry—sorry.
Sarah For goodness' sake. For once in this family, let's try and have a
civilized meal.

*They eat in silence. From a distance Norman is heard singing in the living-
room. Annie, Tom and Reg hear this, catch each other's eyes and then, under
Sarah's withering gaze, continue to eat. As Norman's singing becomes
louder and more boisterous, Annie, Tom and Reg become helpless with stifled
laughter*

C<small>URTAIN</small>

S<small>CENE</small> 2

The same. Sunday, 9 a.m.

*Norman is standing in his pyjamas and bare feet. He is whistling. After a
moment Sarah, in a dressing-gown, enters with a tray of breakfast things
which she takes to the table*

Norman (*cheerfully*) 'Morning.
Sarah (*seeing him*) Oh. (*She unloads the tray, ignoring him*)
Norman Lovely morning. Hear the birds?

Sarah continues grimly with her task

Sleep well? Hope you slept well. I slept well.

Sarah goes out

*Norman starts to whistle again and examines what Sarah has put on the
table*

Annie enters, in a dressing-gown, with another tray of breakfast things

'Morning
Annie (*seeing him*) Oh.

Annie starts unloading her tray, ignoring him

Norman Lovely morning. Sleep well, did you? I slept like a log. Must

have been that wine. Wonderful. It's a rotten drink but it makes a
lovely sleeping draught. I'd market it. Sleep Nature's way with our
dandelion brew. Arhar . . .

*Annie goes out passing Sarah coming in with the last of the breakfast
things*

Norman What have we got for breakfast, then? What have we got?
Sarah (*calling*) Reg! Breakfast.
Reg (*off, distant*) Right . . .

Sarah sits and starts her breakfast

Norman How's old Reg this morning? All right, is he? Sleep well, did
he? I can tell you I can do with some breakfast. Missed my meal last
night. Did you know that? I missed my meal. I didn't hear the dinner
gong. What sort of hotel do you call this?

Annie enters

Sarah Have you taken Mother her's up?
Annie Yes.
Norman I'll sit here, shall I? All right if I sit here? Anybody any objections
if I sit here? (*He is ignored*) I'll sit here.

*Norman sits at the head of the table. Sarah sits at the other end with Annie
close to her, isolating Norman. Norman sits whistling*

Reg enters, dressed in a sports shirt and sandals

Reg (*cheerily*) 'Morning, all.
Norman 'Morning.
Reg (*his face falling*) Oh.

Reg sits next to Sarah. Annie and Reg have cereal. Sarah butters toast

Norman Well, you're a right cheery lot, aren't you? Look at you. A right
cheery lot. Woo-hoo-hallooo . . . (*He waves at them*)
Sarah (*acidly*) Nobody in this house is speaking to you ever again.
Norman Oh, I see. I see. That's the way the Swiss rolls. I see. That's the
way the apple crumbles, is it? Oh ho. That's the way the corn flakes . . .
(*A pause. He ponders. Suddenly—sharply*) Sarah! Be careful! The
butter . . .
Sarah (*alarmed*) What?
Norman Ha-ha! You spoke to me. Caught you. Caught you. (*Pause*) All
right, I'll talk to myself then. (*Very rapidly, in two voices*) Hallo, Norman
—good morning, Norman—how are you, Norman—I'm very well,
Norman—that's good news, Norman . . .
Annie Shut up, Norman.
Norman Ha-ha! Caught you again. That's two of you. Just got to catch

old Reg now. Two out of three. Just Reg left . . . (*Slight pause*) Look out, Reg! (*No reaction*) Ah—can't catch him that way. (*Sharply*) Hey, Reg! Oh well. If that's the way it is. Don't talk to me. I don't care. Doesn't bother me. I don't know why you're all being so unsociable. All right, I had a few drinks last night. What's wrong with that? Hasn't anyone round this table ever had a drink then? Come on, I don't believe it. You've had a drink, haven't you, Reg? Ha-ha! Caught you. You spoke.

Reg No, I didn't.

Norman Ha-ha! Three to me. I've won. (*Pause*) Nothing wrong in a few drinks. Don't speak. I don't care. Going to be a pretty dull Sunday if we all sit in silence, I can tell you. Well, I'm not sitting in silence. I'll find something to do. I know, I'll go up and frighten Mother.

Sarah looks up sharply and gives him a terrible glare

Ah-ha! Nearly got you again. Is it too much to ask for something to eat?

No response

It's too much to ask for something to eat. (*He gets up and moves down the table and takes the cereal bowl that Sarah is not using*) May I borrow your bowl? That's awfully nice of you. And your spoon? Thank you. Now then, what shall I have? (*Examining the cereal packets*) Puffa Puffa Rice. Ah-ha . . . (*He returns to the top of the table, sits and fills his bowl*) No Sunday papers. Dear, dear. Ah, well I shall have to read my morning cereal. (*He laughs*) Cereal. Do we all get that? Apparently we don't. (*He reads. Suddenly violently banging the table*) Stop!

The others jump involuntarily

Stop everything. Listen. A free pair of pinking shears for only seventy-nine p and six Puffa Puffa tokens. Hurry, hurry, hurry. What's this? Is nobody hurrying? Do you mean to tell me that none of you want them? Where's the spirit of British pinking? Dead, presumably. Like my relations. (*He eats a handful of dry cereal thoughtfully*) Hang on, I've got another game. Mind reading. I'll read your minds. Now then, where shall we start? Sarah. Sarah is thinking—that noisy man up there should be home with his wife. What is he doing shattering the calm of our peaceful Sunday breakfast with his offers of reduced price pinking shears. Why is he here, shouting at us like this? Why isn't he at home, like any other decent husband, shouting at his wife? He came down here to seduce his wife's own sister. How low can he get? The fact that his wife's own sister said, at one stage anyway, that she was perfectly happy to go along with him is beside the point. The fact that little Annie here was perfectly happy to ditch old reliable Tom—without a second thought —and come off with me is beside the point. We won't mention that because it doesn't quite fit in with the facts as we would like them. And what is little Annie thinking, I wonder? Maybe furtively admiring my pyjamas, who knows? Pyjamas that could have been hers. With all that they contain. (*He sits*) "These nearly were mine." Or maybe she is thinking, "Phew, that was a close shave. I could be shacked up in some dreadful hotel with this man—at this very moment—what a lucky escape for me. Thank heavens, I am back here at home amidst my talkative family exchanging witty breakfast banter. Knowing my two-legged faithful companion and friend, Tom, the rambling vet, is even now planning to propose to me in nineteen-ninety-seven just as soon as he's cured our cat. Meanwhile, I can live here peacefully, totally fulfilled, racing up and down stairs looking after Mother, having the time of my life and living happily ever after until I'm fifty-five and fat. I'm glad I didn't go to that hotel" Well, let me tell you so am I. I wouldn't want a week-end with you, anyway. And I'll tell you the funniest thing of all, shall I?

Annie gets up and runs out

(*yelling furiously after her*) I didn't even book the hotel. I knew you wouldn't come. You didn't have the guts.

A pause

Sarah You can be very cruel, can't you, Norman?

Sarah goes out after Annie

Norman Oh, well. It's a bit quieter without those two. Hear yourself speak. Too damned noisy before. All that crunching of toast. Like a brigade of Guards marching on gravel. Well now, Reg . . .

Reg chews glumly through his cereal

(*Looking round the table*) Milk? Ah. (*He gets up*) Sugar? (*He returns with these and sits. Pouring milk over his cereal*) Nice peaceful morning. Just the two of us and—hark! the soft crackle of my Puffa Puffa Rice. 'Tis spring indeed. (*Slight pause*) I suppose you think I'm cruel, too, don't you? Well, I've damn good cause to be, haven't I? I mean, nobody's thought about my feelings, have they? It's all Annie—Annie —Annie—what about me? I was going to give her everything. Well, as much as I could. My whole being. I wanted to make her happy for a week-end, that's all. I wanted to give her . . . (*Angrily*) It was only for a few hours for God's sake. Saturday night, back on Monday morning. That was all it was going to be. My God! The fuss. What about your wife, Norman? What about my wife. Don't you think I'd take Ruth away, just the same? If she'd come. But she won't. She has no need of me at all, that woman, except as an emotional punch bag. I tell you, if you gave Ruth a rose, she'd peel all the petals off to make sure there weren't any greenfly. And when she'd done that, she'd turn round and say, do you call that a rose? Look at it, it's all in bits. That's Ruth. If she came in now, she wouldn't notice me. She'd probably hang her coat on me. It's not fair, Reg. Look, I'll tell you. A man with my type of temperament should really be ideally square-jawed, broad-shouldered,

have blue twinkling eyes, a chuckle in his voice and a spring in his stride.
He should get through three women a day without even ruffling his hair.
That's what I'm like inside. That's my appetite. That's me. I'm a three-a-
day man. There's enough of me in here to give. Not just sex, I'm talking
about everything. The trouble is, I was born in the wrong damn body.
Look at me. A gigolo trapped in a haystack. The tragedy of my life.
Norman Dewars, gigolo and assistant librarian. What's inside you,
Reg? Apart from twelve bowls of cornflakes? What do you feel with
Sarah? Do you sometimes feel like saying to her, no, this is me. The
real me. Look at me . . .

Reg finishes his cornflakes

Reg I'll tell you something, Norman. You're a nice bloke. You've got
your faults but you're a nice bloke, but I think you must be the last
person in the world I ever want to have breakfast with again.
Norman Oh.
Reg No hard feelings you understand, but . . .

Sarah enters, looking pleased

Sarah Well, Norman. A little surprise for you.
Norman Oh, yes.
Sarah Someone to see you.
Norman Ruth?
Sarah Just arrived. Isn't that nice? (*Turning to go off, calling*) Ruth!

Sarah goes out to the house

Reg (*alarmed*) Did someone say Ruth? Oh, no . . . (*He rises, snatches a
piece of toast and butters it hastily*)
Norman Tell her I'm not here. Tell her I'm . . .

*Ruth enters. She is yelling the end of a conversation with Annie back in
the kitchen*

Ruth . . . I was pulled right over to the left, there was plenty of room for
him to pass me. He had yards and yards, he just . . . (*Turning into the
room*) Norman? Where is Norman?
Norman Norman is here.
Ruth (*peering short-sightedly*) Norman?—Oh, there you are.
Reg (*buttered toast in hand, heading for the french window*) 'Morning,
Ruth. See you later.

Reg goes out to the garden

Ruth (*continuing as if he was still in the room, fumbling in her bag*) Oh,
Reg, how are you. I've been meaning to ring you but I haven't had a
minute and how are those enchanting kids of yours? Little whatser-
name . . . ?

Norman He's gone.

Ruth (*looking up, peering round the room*) What?

Norman Reg has left the room. He's gone.

Ruth Oh. Well, I was only being polite. I haven't seen him for ages . . .

Norman You haven't seen anyone for ages. Why don't you wear your glasses?

Ruth (*sitting*) Norman, what is going on here? What are you up to?

Norman Since when have you cared what I'm up to?

Ruth Well, I don't normally. You know you're perfectly free to come and go. Not that I could stop you. But I do object to having my Saturday nights ruined by all these bizarre phone calls. First of all, you ringing up screaming drunk—and then Sarah, practically at midnight, simply demanding I come down. Now what is going on?

Norman You don't know?

Ruth No. Is there anything to eat?

Norman Sarah hasn't told you then?

Ruth All she said was that you were here and that I ought to be here, too. She sounded as if she was summoning relatives to your bedside . . .

Norman I suppose she was, in a manner of speaking.

Ruth I got quite worried.

Norman Worried? Hah!

Ruth What's that you're eating?

Norman Since when do you worry about me?

Ruth Of course I do. Now and then. Don't be tiresome. Is that cereal?

Norman Puffa Puffa rice. (*Pushing the bowl to her*) Here, have it. After all you said to me about having no love for me—no feelings for me at all?

Ruth Did I say that?

Norman You know you did.

Ruth No, I didn't.

Norman It's imprinted on my brain . . .

Ruth All I said was—is there any milk and sugar or do I have to eat these dry—all I said was . . .

Norman It's got milk on . . .

Ruth All I said was—that if you were all that unhappy with me—perhaps we ought to think of terminating our marriage . . .

Norman (*excitedly*) Terminating it? You make it sound like a legal contract.

Ruth That's exactly what it is, Norman. Don't be obtuse.

Norman Marriage is more than that!

Ruth Yes, all right, don't shout . . .

Norman Marriage is sharing and giving and—things. Is that how you've seen us for five years? A legal contract? Some marriage. No confetti, please—just throw sealing wax and red tape. Do you take this woman, hereinafter called the licensee of the first party . . .

Ruth Norman, I can't go into all this now. Is there any sugar on this table?

Norman And this man, hereinafter called the donor and sole giver . . .

Ruth Norman, darling, do see if you can find the sugar.

Norman (*rising and assembling everything in sight around Ruth*) Here. Tea, toast, marmalade, butter, knife, spoon, cup, saucer, hot water, sugar. All right?

Ruth Thank you.

Norman (*sinking back in a chair*) I don't think there's any hope for us. We're doomed.

Ruth Norman. Can we talk quietly, please.

Norman I doubt it.

Ruth This is a perfect opportunity. We're on our own. We can sit here, talk, listen to each other's point of view and try and sort things out. (*She picks up the hot water jug*)

Norman (*making an effort*) All right. All right. I'll try. (*With sudden suppressed anger*) You are pouring hot water on your Puffa Puffa rice.

Ruth (*absently*) What?

Norman I told you they had milk on already. Why do you do that? You're always doing that. Why don't you look what you're doing?

Ruth It doesn't matter.

Norman If you'd only wear your glasses.

Ruth I don't need glasses to eat cornflakes. I can see perfectly well, thank you. I just wasn't concentrating . . .

Norman We're incompatible. We're damn well incompatible.

Ruth I can see as well as you. It's only people I sometimes can't see very clearly.

Norman Our house is knee deep in unused pairs of glasses.

Ruth And most of the time that's preferable.

Norman It's like a sale at an optician's.

Ruth Norman . . .

Norman Thousands of pairs of glasses.

Ruth (*angrily*) Norman! (*Taking a breath, calmly now*) I have a great deal of work I should be doing at home. I have given that up. I have come down here because I was asked to come. I did not want to come. I want to stay as short a time as possible. Is that clear?

Norman Oh, yes. Got to get back to your work.

Ruth Yes, I do. I have two full reports that have to be in tomorrow. If they are not in, I shall proably be fired. If I'm fired, we will have no money to pay the mortgage, no money for three quarters of the gas and electricity bills . . .

Norman All right, I'm a kept man. A married ponce.

Ruth I don't mind keeping you. Not in the least. But I cannot continually chase after you all over the countryside. I just cannot spare the time, I'm sorry. As it is, you've held my career back about ten years. You interrupt me at meetings with embarrassing phone calls . . .

Norman To tell you I love you, that's all. Is that wrong?

Ruth You're continually bursting into my office when I'm seeing clients . . .

Norman My God, is it wrong to love your wife?

Ruth You behave abominably when I bring business friends home to dinner . . .

Norman (*snarling*) What do they know about love?

Ruth You have even been known to scrawl obscenities over my business papers.

Norman All right, all right. I love you. I'm sorry.

Ruth Yes, I love you too, Norman, but please leave me alone.

Norman All right. In future, I'll whisper it quietly from Brazil. Would that suit you?

Ruth All I'm saying is, please try and see my point of view. Try and consider me.

Norman I feel trapped. I'm a captive husband. That's what I am. (*He sinks his head in his hands*)

Ruth I have an awful feeling we haven't made much progress on that topic. Let's try another. What have you been doing down here to upset Sarah? I thought you had a conference.

Norman Hah!

Ruth Have you made a pass at her or something? Well, you'd better come home with me. You're not wanted here quite obviously. You can come home and mow the lawn.

Norman Mow the lawn . . . Do you want to know what I'm doing here? I'll tell you, shall I?

Ruth If you want to.

Norman I will tell you. (*He rises*)

Ruth Where are you going?

Norman Nowhere. I'm just standing up.

Ruth Well, sit down, I can't see you properly.

Norman This has to be said standing up.

Ruth What is it, the National Anthem?

Norman All right, you've had this coming . . . (*He pauses dramatically*)

Ruth Anyway, I discovered that they're what made me sneeze.

Norman What are?

Ruth My glasses. Whenever I wear them, I sneeze and my eyes run, so I can't see anything with them on anyway. I think they press on my sinus passages.

Norman Vanity, that's what it is.

Ruth It is not vanity. I am not vain.

Norman Staring at yourself in the mirror all day long. Tarting yourself up for these so-called business associates.

Ruth And I do not stare at myself in the mirror. For one thing I can't see myself properly without my glasses, and because I can't bear looking at myself in glasses because I look so terrible in them, I never look at myself at all.

Norman Do you want to hear what I have to say or don't you?

Ruth Yes, all right. Just don't say I'm vain.

Norman It concerns you, you know.

Ruth It usually does.

Norman There is someone else.

Ruth What?

Norman Whilst you have been engrossed in your financial wizardry— rigging the books for corrupt capitalist companies . . .

Ruth Norman . . .

Norman I very nearly, but for the grace of God and unforseen circumstances, went off with another woman.

Ruth You did?

Norman Yes.

Ruth Seriously?

Norman Yes. I thought better of it in time. Thank heavens. Told her, I wouldn't. But that was the reason behind this week-end. We had planned to go off together.

Ruth For good?

Norman No—probably not . . .

Ruth Well, for how long?

Norman Till Monday.

Ruth Oh, I see. I thought you were a bit odd lately.

Norman Odd?

Ruth Well—quieter than usual. Who was it you were going with?

Norman Does it matter?

Ruth No. Since you didn't even go.

Norman Do you want to know?

Ruth Not if you don't want to tell me.

Pause

Norman You want to know though, don't you?

Ruth No, not really.

Pause

Norman I'll tell you, shall I?

Ruth You might as well.

Norman Annie.

Ruth Annie?

Norman Yes.

Ruth Oh, Norman . . .

Norman I thought that would shake you.

Ruth I don't think I even believe you.

Norman It's true.

Ruth Not Annie. She's far too sensible.

Norman We had planned a week-end together.

Ruth You and Annie?

Norman (*irritated*) Yes.

Ruth Where?

Norman East Grinstead.

Ruth (*staring at him a second and then bursting into laughter*) Oh, my God . . .

Norman Don't laugh. It's true.

Annie enters with a tray

Just the two of us together.

Ruth (*laughing uncontrollably*) I have never heard anything so funny.

Annie I'll clear this later, I'm sorry . . .

Norman Annie! (*To Ruth*) Why won't you believe me? We were going away—together . . . (*Grabbing Annie*) Annie, you tell her, you tell her . . . You'd have lost me for ever, do you know that?

Annie (*pulling away*) Oh, Norman . . .

Ruth (*drying her eyes*) I'm sorry—it's just East Grinstead . . . (*She starts laughing again*)

Norman All right, go on, laugh. We're in love.

Norman strides across to Annie seizes her and her tray rather awkwardly and clasps her to him

Don't you care? We're in love . . .

Sarah comes in with a second tray. She stops in the doorway

Annie (*struggling, muffled as she is clasped to Norman's bosom*) Norman, don't . . .

Norman We're in love . . .

Ruth continues to laugh. Sarah surveying the scene, looks on horrified

CURTAIN

ACT II

SCENE 1

The same. Sunday, 8 p.m.

Annie is discovered putting knives and forks away in the sideboard. Norman creeps in

Norman (*in a whisper*) Annie.
Annie (*jumping*) Oh, don't do that. Frightened me to death.
Norman (*whispering*) Hallo.
Annie (*whispering*) Hallo. What are you doing?
Norman (*whispering*) Wanted to see you alone.
Annie (*whispering*) Why are we whispering?
Norman (*whispering*) Them.
Annie (*normally*) They can't hear us.
Norman (*loudly*) Oh, Annie, I need you. (*He moves to her*)
Annie Ssh. (*She pulls away*) Norman . . .
Norman What's wrong?
Annie Nothing. Just don't . . .
Norman Why not? Have you gone off me?
Annie Well, slightly—no. You know . . .
Norman What do you mean, slightly?
Annie (*confused*) Oh . . .
Norman What?
Annie Well, it's ridiculous now. Tom's here. Ruth's here. Stop playing games.
Norman Oh, it's a game now, is it? When we planned this week-end it was no game. It was going to be an adventure. An experience for both of us.
Annie But we didn't plan to spend it here, did we? Anyway, it's all gone wrong. Everybody knows, including Ruth.
Norman Ruth? I wouldn't worry about her. She laughed. Can you imagine that, laughing . . .
Annie She was right. It was absurd. I don't think Tom's laughing, mind you.
Norman Tom. Who cares what he thinks.
Annie I do.
Norman You do?
Annie Yes.
Norman I thought he didn't matter to you.
Annie I never said that.
Norman You implied . . .

Annie No.

Norman What about me? I mean, us?

Annie (*sharply*) What about us, Norman?

Norman I see. That's me finished with, is it? As far as you're concerned. Chucked away like an empty bottle. That's my lot.

Annie Yes.

Norman God, you're cruel.

Annie Yes.

Norman I expect it's because of last night, isn't it?

Annie Not really.

Norman That's why you're angry with me. Because I got drunk. But I got drunk because of you, don't you see? I was unhappy so I got drunk. I'm sorry.

Annie Doesn't bother me.

Norman I got disgustingly drunk.

Annie You can get as drunk as you like, it doesn't bother me.

Norman Oh, great. Would you mind if I dropped dead?

Annie That's entirely up to you.

Norman Oh, fine. That's fine. (*He ponders*) You're getting bitter. Did you know that? You used to be innocent and pure and fragile.

Annie Oh, balls. I'm sorry, Norman, but balls. You do talk rubbish. No-one can spend five years looking after that cantankerous woman upstairs and remain innocent and pure. And after lugging her in and out of bed single-handed, day in day out, I'm the last person in this world you'd call fragile. I mean, look at me, Norman, do I look even remotely fragile?

Norman I meant mentally fragile.

Annie That sounds even worse. Makes me sound like a half-wit.

Norman I don't know what's got into you. You've been corrupted.

Annie I'm sick to death of being used, Norman.

Norman I think I must have corrupted you, somehow.

Annie You and Ruth will have to play on your own. Don't use me as ammunition.

Norman And cynical. I never thought you'd get like that. I think it's my fault. (*Pause*) So you're going back to Tom?

Annie I'm not going back to anyone. I just want to be left alone. I've had you shoving me, Sarah shoving me, Ruth sniggering. I'll be glad when you've all gone home. I really will. I'm sorry.

Norman I think I've got one of my depressions coming on again. I came in here for comfort.

Annie Well, go and see Ruth.

Norman All right. Back to the living death, eh?

Annie Oh, Norman. You make me so angry.

Norman All right. I'll go. I know when I'm not wanted. I'll go back where I'm not wanted. I'll go. Good-bye.

Annie (*infuriated, picking up the biscuit tin threateningly*) I warn you I'll . . .

Norman Go on. Go on. What have I got to live for?

Annie screams in frustration. She bangs down the tin

Tom enters from the garden

Tom Ah.
Annie Hallo, Tom.
Tom Hallo.

They stand for a moment in silence

Norman Well, I can see I'm in the way. If you'll excuse me, I'm just off to look for a length of rope.
Annie You are not in anyone's way but your own. I'm going to start dinner. Excuse me both of you.

Annie goes out to the house

Norman It must be your after-shave.
Tom Um?
Norman That drives them away.
Tom Oh. Look here, Norman. You're a very good fellow.
Norman Thank you.
Tom I've always thought of you as a good fellow. However. This is difficult to say without hurting your feelings. I don't think you're a very good influence on Annie.
Norman Really?
Tom I've heard all about this business of your going away. I've also observed you this week-end. I don't think I like it at all. It's upsetting her and that's not right. The point is, if it happens again—well, I used to do boxing. I didn't enjoy it and I wasn't at all good. I couldn't get out of it, you see. It was compulsory at our school. But I did learn to throw a pretty useful punch. So . . .
Norman Am I being threatened?
Tom Yes.
Norman My God, I'm being threatened . . .

Sarah comes in from the house, with a duster

I am being threatened.
Sarah About time.
Norman Hah!
Sarah (*calling*) Reg!
Tom Excuse me.

Tom goes out to the garden

Norman That man's turned homicidal.
Sarah (*polishing the table*) I think as far as you're concerned, we all have to a certain extent, Norman.

Norman Sarah. You don't hate me, do you? I mean, I know perhaps you disapprove but you don't hate me.

Sarah No, I don't hate you, Norman.

Norman Thank you. Thank you for that, at least.

Sarah But I can't say I like you very much, most of the time.

Norman All right. All right, I'm going . . .

Sarah Norman.

Norman What?

Sarah Will you do something for me?

Norman What?

Sarah Will you try, just for this evening, not to start any more scenes or arguments?

Norman Me?

Sarah (*still polishing away*) I'd like, just for once, all of us to get through an evening—as a family. I don't know if you've realized it, Norman, but I have had a lot of nervous trouble in the past. And every time I come down here, I have a relapse. When I get home from this house, I find I'm shaking all over. For days. And I get these rashes up the insides of my arms.

Norman My goodness.

Sarah Now it's not fair on me, Norman. I have a family to look after, a house to run.

Norman Yes, yes of course.

Sarah Well.

Norman Yes. Your trouble is you're over-emotional.

Sarah Very possibly.

Norman You're like me.

Sarah Are you sure I am?

Norman We feel. We've got nerve-endings sticking out of our heads. We've no cynicism or scepticism to act as shock absorbers. Everything that is, that happens becomes part of us. We're probably a new race. Had you thought of that? Born too early.

Sarah All I'm saying is, if there's too much noise, I get these headaches.

Norman We're not understood. None of that lot out there understand us. They're all bogged down in their own little lives.

Sarah Yes . . .

Norman Self obsessed. Annie, Tom, Ruth—even Reg. Don't worry, Sarah.

Sarah What?

Norman This evening's going to be all right.

Sarah Is it?

Norman We'll both go flat out together to make it a success.

Sarah Oh, yes?

Norman For God's sake, this is a family. We should care. If we don't care, brothers, sisters, husbands, wives—if we can't finally join hands, what hope is there for anybody. Make it a banquet, Sarah my love, make it a banquet.

Sarah There's nothing in the larder.

Norman Improvise. We can improvise. What do we need? (*He rushes to* *the sideboard and grabs handfuls of cutlery indiscriminately from the drawer)* Knives—forks—spoons . . . (*He scatters them on the table)*

Sarah Yes, all right, Norman, I'll do it.

Norman (*producing linen*) Table napkins.

Sarah No, Norman, those are traycloths. (*She starts to lay the table*) I'll do it, don't worry, please.

Norman All right. I've started you off, I'll leave it to you. I'll go and change.

Sarah Change?

Norman For dinner.

Sarah Change into what?

Norman I'll find something. I'll improvise, Sarah, improvise. It's like an old clothes shop upstairs.

Sarah Annie should have cleared it out. There's her father's clothes still in the wardrobe. There'll be moths.

Norman Quite right.

Norman goes to the door and passes Reg coming in

'Evening, Reg, old sport.

Norman slaps Reg on the back and exits

Reg What's up with him?

Sarah Oh, there you are. (*She replaces the cloths, then continues to set out the cutlery*)

Reg He's very cheerful. That looks ominous.

Sarah I think I've persuaded him to make an effort this evening. I think I have. Would you see if you can find the mats in the drawer.

Reg What sort of effort? (*He looks for the mats*)

Sarah To avoid hysterical scenes. To behave in a civilized manner.

Reg (*at the sideboard*) Ha—ha—ha.

Sarah I pray that for once we might get through the evening without one angry word. I want us to have a quiet meal, to be able to go into the lounge afterwards, sit down all six of us and enjoy each other's company like a family. (*She fetches glasses, napkins and side plates from the sideboard*)

Reg Are you aware who the six people are? Norman to name but five. And Ruth. That's a civil war to start with. Don't ask for the impossible. Just pray we're still alive tomorrow morning. That'll do for a start.

Sarah (*laying the table*) I mean, if a family can't care about each other, what hope is there for the rest of the—I'll never forgive you if you don't try. I mean it, Reg. I know you find it all very amusing—Ruth and Norman continually bickering, Annie behaving like a tramp . . . (*She folds the napkins into a "shape"*)

Reg What?

Sarah You've seen how she's been dressed all day. Tarted up like that, it doesn't suit her, it never did.

Reg You're always on she doesn't bother.

Sarah She doesn't have to go the other way, does she? Why can't she wear something nice and simple and—plain . . . ? All that make-up on. I mean, it's not even fashionable. Especially when you know who she's done it for.

Reg Tom, I should think.

Sarah Tom. For Norman. She's set her sights at him and he's enjoying every minute of it. Playing one sister off against the other . . . Well, any more of this and you know what'll happen? What always happens when I come down here.

Reg Oh, no? You've not got the shakes again, have you?

Sarah You ought to know me by now, Reg. I can't bear these sort of atmospheres.

Reg It's not your back, is it?

Sarah Not at the moment. But the way I've had to run round trying to cope with one crisis after another . . .

Reg Well, sit down. Have a rest for a second.

Sarah (*snapping*) How can I sit down? Be sensible. How can I possibly sit down?

Reg (*snapping back*) All right, stand up. Suit yourself. I'm only trying to be . . . You want these mats?

Sarah Yes, I said I did.

Reg (*studying them*) Marvellous, these are, every picture tells a story.

Sarah (*taking the mats and setting them out*) We're going to need two more chairs. I'm sure there used to be six of these. Heaven knows what she's done with them.

Reg All right, I'll look for chairs. Don't worry, keep calm. It'll be all right.

Annie enters

Annie Well, I've scraped together what there is. It should just about feed us all. Opened every tin we had and poured them into a saucepan. Made a sort of gluey stew. Then there's the salad we can finish . . .

Reg Oh, good grief. Not again.

Annie It works out about one lettuce leaf each.

Reg Thank heaven for that.

Sarah Well done. Didn't you have six of these chairs at one time? I'm sure at Christmas . . .

Annie Oh, yes, they fell to bits.

Sarah Fell to bits?

Annie Everything does that in this house. Woodworm or old age.

Reg You should get that treated.

Annie Old age, you mean?

Reg Ah well, I don't know about that. Father used to say, the only thing for old age is a brave face, a good tailor and comfortable shoes. Chairs . . .

Annie I should use the ones in the sitting-room. There's a couple there with legs.
Reg Right.

Reg goes out

Annie You're using the mats.
Sarah Yes, I thought we'd . . .
Annie Bit posh. We only use those on Mother's birthday.
Sarah Well, I thought we'd do something a little special since we're all here. Nice that Ruth could come.
Annie Yes.
Sarah It makes it complete. And it means that Norman won't be left out.
Annie Yes
Sarah I really do like that dress.
Annie Thank you. It's pretty old but it's a good standby.
Sarah Yes. Anyway, I thought we'd have a really cosy family meal together. Try and make it a happy evening.
Annie Super.

Reg enters with a chair which he places down R *of table*

Reg Here's one of them.
Sarah We need two.
Reg All right, all right. I'm going back for the other. Tom's sitting on it.
Sarah Well, move him off it.
Reg (*going out*) You ever tried moving, Tom?

Reg goes out as Ruth enters

Ruth Somebody's saucepan seems to be getting rather agitated out there.
Sarah Did you turn it down?
Ruth No. I whispered soothing words to it. Of course, I turned it down.
Annie I'll see to it.
Sarah All right. I'll go. I'll go. (*With a glare at Ruth*) If you want something doing in this house, you might as well do it yourself.

Sarah goes out

Ruth My God, Mother's mats. Is it a birth, a death or a marriage?
Annie She's doing the lot. I mean, she's not actually doing anything but she's organizing the lot.
Ruth What on earth for, silly cow? Who's going to notice?
Annie I think this is her attempt at a grand reunion. A cosy family meal with Sarah presiding.
Ruth Oh, no. Have we all got to sit round with fixed grins? It's Christmas all over again. I thought I'd come in here, so I wouldn't embarrass your fiancé or whatever he is. He can't bear to look me in the face.

Annie Poor Tom.

Ruth It was rather unfortunate. Believe it or not, I was attempting un-successfully to give him lessons on how to woo you. Tom being Tom assumed I was giving him lessons on how to woo me. I managed to load him all right but I pointed him in the wrong direction. It was silly of me to interfere, I'm sorry. Serves me right. I'll leave it to Sarah in future. I mean, I don't know you may not even care for the man. You've never really said one way or the other. We've always assumed you and Tom, Tom and you. Presumably you wouldn't have him round here at all if you didn't. You do like him, don't you?

Annie Yes. I'm very fond of him.

Ruth I think he's in love with you. As far as one can fathom. It's just he's so—well, one could be nice and say deep. Except if you say someone's deep, it more or less implies there's something at the bottom. I'm not so sure with Tom.

Annie Oh, you'd be surprised.

Ruth All he needs is a shove. Somebody needs to do it. Anybody. Except Norman, that is. Whose sole advice to Tom was to throw punches at you.

Annie Norman told him to do that?

Ruth It's Norman's answer to female psychology. He's very subtle. Have you noticed? Well, you probably have. You nearly fell for it.

Annie I'm sorry. I never for a minute intended to take Norman away from you or anything.

Ruth Forget it. You couldn't possibly take Norman away from me. That assumes I own him in the first place. I've never done that. I always feel with Norman that I have him on loan from somewhere. Like one of his library books. I'll get a card one day informing me he's overdue and there's a fine to pay on him. Oh, I should have gone back to town this afternoon. I'm going to have to phone the office tomorrow and plead illness. Again. Of all the working days lost in this country over the year, half are due to strikes and illness and the other half to people chasing after Norman.

Reg comes in with the other chair, which has a low seat. He places it up L of table

Reg Got it. He moved. Tom moved. Got the chair.

Ruth Have you seen Norman? I don't like it when I can't see him. Where is he?

Reg Oh, he was shouting about out there. Said something about going up to change.

Annie He's got nothing to change into.

Ruth That won't stop him. He'll probably come down in a counterpane.

Annie Oh, goodness . . . (*She starts to go out*)

Reg whistles. Annie stops and turns to Ruth
  Would you . . .

Ruth I'll try . . .

Ruth goes out, passing Sarah returning with a bottle of home-made wine

Sarah Don't go too far away, Ruth. Nearly ready. I've left the stew to simmer, Annie. Reg, would you call everyone. Tom and Norman.
Reg Right you are. (*Going to the door and yelling*) Tom! Norman!
Sarah (*wincing*) Please, there's no need to shout. Go and fetch them.
Reg Sorry. (*Whispering*) Tom. Norman.
Sarah Reg . . .
Reg All right. All right . . .

Reg goes out. Tom comes in from the garden

Tom Somebody call? (*Sighting the table*) Aha, this looks promising.
Sarah Nearly ready.
Tom Very smart. Napkins, mats, wine—so on.
Sarah And tonight, that wine is strictly rationed.
Tom Ah.
Sarah If you could open it, Tom, it would be most helpful.

Sarah goes out

Tom Right. (*He starts to pull the cork*) Two meals in two days. Not doing badly, am I?
Annie About average.
Tom I think I've sorted things out with Norman.
Annie Have you?
Tom Sent him off with a flea in his ear, I'm afraid.
Annie Oh. Tom . . .
Tom Um?
Annie We've all made a sort of agreement that we're going to try and not have any rows or anything tonight. It's for Sarah's sake really. A really happy meal, you know. So do your bit, won't you?
Tom What, you mean jokes and things?
Annie No, not necessarily.
Tom Oh, good. I'm awfully bad at jokes. I forget the ending.
Annie No, well—I know you never do—but don't complain or cause any trouble, will you?
Tom Lord, no. Just get my food down me. That's all I'm here for. You know me.
Annie (*doubtfully*) Yes . . .

Sarah enters with a tray of plates adorned with sparse salad, which she puts on the sideboard

Sarah Come along. It's all ready. Where is everyone? (*Calling*) Reg . . .

Reg enters from the garden

Reg Can't find either of them. (*Seeing Tom*) Ah, there you are.
Tom Hello, Reg.
Reg No sign of Norman, he's vanished.
Sarah Well, all right, we won't wait. Let's get seated. Reg, you go up the
end there, would you?
Reg Up the end. (*He sits* R *end of the table*)
Sarah And Tom, you come next to me here, would you? (*She indicates
the chair up* L)

Tom walks to the down L *chair and pulls it out*

 Ruth enters

Ruth Norman's in the bathroom.
Sarah Oh well . . .
Ruth From the sound of it, he's washing. He's so ashamed of the fact
he's locked the door. (*She sits in the chair Tom has pulled out*)
Sarah Oh well, he'll be down I expect—no, not there, Ruth dear. Would
you mind sitting one seat further up?

Ruth moves to the chair down R *and sits*

Ruth (*moving grudgingly*) Oh, really . . .
Annie Where am I sitting?
Sarah (*to Tom who has sat on chair vacated by Ruth down* L *and unfolded
napkin*) You're here, Tom. (*Indicating the chair up* L) Sit here.

*Tom rises and moves to sit, unfolding the napkin. He does not sit on this low
chair until the end of the sequence*

Reg (*offering Annie his own chair*) Annie, you should be sitting here.
You're the hostess.
Annie (*sitting*) Right.
Sarah No, she can't sit there. She's out of order.
Reg She's the hostess. She should sit at the head.
Sarah But then we've got two women sitting together.
Ruth (*indicating down* L *chair*) I'll move back down here then. That's easy
enough.
Sarah (*stopping her*) No, Ruth, no. Stay where you are.
Reg Now I'll go here next to Annie. Then it's right. (*He sits up* R)
Tom No, it's not. You're next to me.
Sarah (*getting agitated*) Now, we've got two men together. Why don't
you leave it to me?
Reg It's all right, it's all right. Don't get excited. Now, Tom, you move
round one and sit at the end there.

Sarah moves to the down L *place, refolding the napkin*

Tom (*going to do so*) Right-ho. (*He sits* L *and unfolds a napkin*)
Ruth Would it be easier if I ate in the kitchen?
Reg Just a second. Do you mind, Ruth, do you mind.
Sarah Don't sit there, Tom. That's my chair.
Tom Oh, I'm sorry, I thought he said . . . (*He moves one chair further round
and unfolds a napkin*)

Reg Now, we want a girl over here. Ruth. Over here.
Ruth (*moving round the table to above it*) I don't want to worry you but you've got a woman at both ends of the table.
Sarah That's what I'm saying. Why won't you listen?
Reg No, no, look. We've got Ruth, there—then me—then Annie—Norman over there, when he comes and Tom next to—ah, that's where we're wrong. Tom, you're in the wrong seat.
Tom (*jumping up guiltily*) Sorry. I thought she said . . .
Ruth (*moving back to the chair down* R) I am about to sit down permanently.
Sarah Reg, will you listen.
Reg Tom, you're supposed to be at the end.
Sarah Reg . . .
Tom I've just been moved from there.
Ruth I am sitting down—now. (*She sits*)
Reg Look, do as you're told and go to the end.

Tom sits L *immediately behind Sarah and unfolds a napkin*

Sarah (*screaming*) Reg, will you kindly leave this to me.
Reg I am simply trying . . .
Annie (*hissing*) Reg.
Reg What? All right, love, all right. I leave it to you. I was only trying to help. Everybody, go where Sarah tells them.
Sarah Thank you. Tom. (*She glances round the table unable to find him. Then, discovering him behind her, angrily*) You are sitting here.
Tom Aha. Back where I started. (*He sits up* L)
Sarah Reg, at the top.
Reg (*sitting*) That's wrong, you know . . .
Sarah At the top. Ruth.
Ruth I have sat down. I refuse to get up.
Annie (*hissing*) Ruth.
Sarah Ruth, you're all right where you are.

Norman enters, now dressed in an old ill-fitting suit and collar and a floppy tie. His jacket has a row of medals on it

Norman 'Evening.
Sarah (*aghast*) Norman.

Reg laughs. Sarah glares. Annie takes two plates from the sideboard for Sarah and Tom

Annie Ssh.

Reg stops laughing

Norman I heard we were dressing for dinner. Good evening. Carry on, talk among yourselves.

Norman sits between Reg at the top of the table and Tom, who is on the very low chair

Sarah No, Norman, not there.
Reg Is that my father's suit you've got on?
Norman If he was a man with extraordinary arm and inside leg measurements, yes indeed.

Annie takes plates to Norman and Reg

Sarah Norman, not there.
Norman Why not here?
Annie (*hissing*) Norman.
Sarah Because it's wrong.
Norman Wrong? Is it wrong to sit between my old pal Reg and this dwarf on my left? (*Patting the top of Tom's head*) Hallo, little chap.
Tom Hallo.
Ruth (*hissing*) Norman.
Sarah Norman!
Annie It's all right, Sarah. I'll sit here. It's fine.
Sarah But . . .

Annie brings plates for Ruth and herself and sits down L of the table

Annie This is fine.
Reg Fine.
Ruth Fine.
Tom Fine.
Sarah Oh, well. It's not correct. (*She sits L of the table*)
Norman Is this lettuce leaf all for me? I can hardly believe my good fortune.
Annie (*hissing*) Norman.

A pause

Sarah Well . . .

A pause

Reg (*suddenly*) Talking of animals . . .

People look up in surprise

Another amusing story about a vet for you, Tom.
Tom Oh.
Reg There's this Englishman and this Italian, you see, standing by a lake.
Norman That's unusual.
Reg And, anyway, they see this dog fall in the water, you see—nearly drowning—coughing and spluttering—nearly drowning.
Norman Woof—splutter splutter—woof woof.
Reg Thank you, Norman. Yes. Well, the Italian dives in, rescues the dog, brings it back to the shore, lays it out, gives it mouth-to-mouth respiration . . .
Norman Uggh.
Reg Twenty seconds, the dog's perfectly all right. The Englishman says,

that's wonderful. Are you a vet? The Italian says, am I a vet? I'm a-soaking vet, what do you think? (*He laughs*)

Norman laughs. The others manage faint smiles. Silence

Norman I liked that. Subtle foreign joke. Did you get that, Tom?
Tom Yes, I think so.
Norman Thought it might have been above your head. (*He laughs*)
Annie (*hissing*) Norman.
Norman Above your head . . .
Ruth Norman.

Ruth aims a kick at Norman but kicks Reg. Reg jumps

I'm sorry.
Norman (*rising*) This lettuce is superb. Whoever cooked this has a knack with lettuce. It's a triumph. Thank you. (*He sits*)

A pause

Sarah Are you all right there, Tom? You're terribly low.
Tom No, I'm fine.
Sarah Do you want to fetch a . . . ?
Tom (*anxiously*) No, no, no.
Sarah We've been very lucky with the weather.
All Yes.
Norman True, true. (*Pause*) Could have been raining, couldn't it?
Sarah Yes.

A pause

Norman Or even snowing. (*Pause*) Snow in July. Unusual but you never know these days, do you? I mean, we must be thankful for small mercies, in my opinion. If this was Australia, this would be mid-winter. Think of that. Thick snow on the koolibah trees, koala bears rushing about in gum boots . . .
Ruth Norman, just sit quietly and enjoy your lettuce.
Norman (*in an undertone*) I'm making small talk.
Ruth Yes. Well, it's not quite small enough, dear.
Norman I can't get it any smaller. I'll swallow it.

A pause

Tom Excuse me . . .
Sarah Yes, Tom.
Tom Er—salt.
Sarah Pass Tom the salt, Norman.
Norman Salt. Certainly. Here we are, little fellow. You enjoying eating with the grown-ups, are you? Long past your bedtime.
Tom Oh, do put a bun in it, Norman, there's a good chap.
Norman A bun. I should be so lucky.
Sarah Why don't you get a cushion, Tom?
Tom (*irritably*) No.

Sarah All right, all right. I was only suggesting . . .
Tom Sorry.

A pause

Annie Everyone finished? I'll get the rest. (*She rises and starts to stack
plates*)
Sarah Tom hasn't quite finished.
Tom All right, all right. Don't worry about me.
Ruth Do you mean to say there's more?
Annie Just some stew so called.
Ruth Well, I'll try and squeeze it in.
Annie Look, if you want to take over and try and do any better . . .
Ruth All right, sorry.
Annie Sitting there on your backside complaining.
Ruth Who's complaining. It's a feast.
Sarah (*shrilly*) Don't let's quarrel, please.
Reg Plates. Let's have the plates, everybody.

*Reg stacks his, Ruth's and Norman's plates and gives them to Annie.
Norman takes Tom's plate as he is about to take a mouthful of lettuce*

Annie Thank you. Won't be a second. (*She starts to go*)
Tom Annie . . . (*He holds out his knife and fork*)

   Annie pauses to take Tom's knife and fork, then goes out

Sarah (*in a low whisper*) Reg . . .
Reg Mm?
Sarah (*quietly*) Offer to help.
Norman (*loudly*) Offer to help.
Reg Oh, all right. Does she need it?
Sarah She's doing it all on her own.
Reg All right.

   Reg goes out

Sarah Now, would somebody like to pour us some wine?
Norman (*rising to do so*) Certainly. Certainly. My pleasure . . .
Ruth This meal is rapidly becoming unbearable.
Norman (*offering wine*) Sarah?
Sarah Just a little drop. Thank you, Norman.

Norman continues pouring wine around the table

Ruth Why don't you take a tranquillizer and go to bed, Sarah. Leave us
to fight in peace.
Sarah Because there is no reason to fight.
Ruth None of us happen to like each other very much. I think that's a
a very good reason.

Norman Speak for yourself. I am full of love this evening.
Ruth Just for yourself? Or is anyone else included?
Sarah Ignore her, Norman, ignore her.
Norman I will, Sarah, I will.
Tom Ah!
Norman (*sitting again, to Tom*) Hallo, Junior.
Tom I just remembered it. A joke.
Ruth Oh, God.
Sarah Oh, a joke, Tom. That's nice.
Tom Quite a funny one, really.
Norman I prefer those.
Sarah Go on, Tom.
Tom Er—well—it's about these two missionaries. And they're in Africa, you see and—no, three missionaries, sorry—and they were . . .
Sarah In Africa, yes.
Tom I think it was Africa. Doesn't really matter, really. Anyway . . .

Annie enters carrying the stew in a saucepan followed by Reg with a pile of soup plates: they put them on the table

Annie Here we are. Thought we'd better use soup plates. It's very runny. It's mostly tinned soup, anyway.

Reg sits

Sarah Couldn't you have used the dish?
Annie This is all right. Nobody minds a saucepan. Just more washing up otherwise. Do you want to dish up or shall I?
Sarah No, no, that's all right.
Tom And there was this tribe of very wild cannibals.
Annie Cannibals? Where?
Tom In Africa, I think.
Annie What's he talking about?
Ruth He's telling us a joke.
Annie Oh, no, Tom love, you don't need to. Honestly.
Norman It's a funny one.
Sarah Quiet. Let Tom tell his joke.
Annie (*starting to dish up*) I hope there's enough to go round.
Tom And the first missionary says, look here, I'm going to try and convert these very wild cannibals to Christianity. You see. And off he goes—through the jungle . . .
Annie (*to Tom*) Can you pass this to Reg?
Norman Good health, friends.
Tom Through the jungle—for days and days . . .
Annie (*handing a plate to Ruth*) Ruth.
Reg What are these white lumps?
Annie Tinned potatoes, probably.
Reg Oh.
Could be tinned pears. I lost count.

Tom And eventually he comes to this village which is full of these very wild cannibals dancing about . . .

Norman Woolla—woolla—woolla.

Annie That's for Norman. I hope it's hot enough.

Ruth What on earth do you call this?

Annie Sloppy stew. Take it or leave it. Tom . . .

Tom (*taking his plate*) Thank you very much. And as soon as they see him, they grab hold of him and put him in the cooking pot.

Norman This is a very tall story for a short man.

Annie Sarah—oh, I've run out. I gave Reg too much. Reg . . .

Ruth You can have mine.

Annie No, I gave Reg too much. Pass your plate down, Reg.

Reg Ah. Some more is there?

Norman No. Less.

Reg Less?

Annie I miscalculated. Sorry.

Reg Well, I didn't get all that much.

Sarah You had more than anybody else. Pass your plate.

Reg passes his plate back

I'm sorry, you were saying, Tom?

Tom Yes. And the chief of these very wild cannibals says . . .

Annie shares out Reg's helping

Annie Sorry, Reg, fair shares for all.

Ruth You're welcome to mine.

Reg We're in no danger of overeating.

Reg's plate is passed back. Annie sits

Tom I think I'm giving this story up.

Sarah You eat far too much, anyway. Do you good.

Tom Nobody seems to be listening.

Norman I'm listening, little friend.

Reg I'll be glad to get home for a meal.

Sarah It's all right for you, you don't have to cook it, do you. Think of me for a change . . .

Annie This isn't bad, considering. Like oxtail soup with unidentified lumps.

Sarah Think of it as a rest for me. I mean, what rest do I get at home. Not only you to look after but the children as well.

Ruth If you didn't want children, you shouldn't have had them.

Sarah I never said I didn't want them, Ruth.

Ruth You're always making out they're some dreadful burden. Like a penance. You never seem to enjoy them.

Sarah It's very difficult to talk to someone who's never had any children.

Ruth Through choice. Through choice.

Norman Your choice.

Ruth Certainly my choice.

Sarah And very one-sided it is by the sound of it.

Ruth No more than yours probably was. I mean, did you honestly consult Reg as to whether he wanted children?

Sarah Of course, I did.

Annie Biologically impossible not to, I should think.

Reg and Norman laugh

Ruth I simply cannot bear this blind pig-headed assumption that you're a totally unfulfilled second class woman until you've had children.

Sarah I never said that.

Norman May I say a word here?

Ruth You imply it. You use those children like some awful weapon. I alone who have borne children know the true meaning of suffering.

Norman Hear! Hear!

Sarah I don't know what you're talking about. That's absolute nonsense. I mean, it's no business of mine if you choose to deny yourself one of the greatest satisfactions . . .

Ruth There you go again. Denying myself. What's the matter with the woman.

Reg Hey, hey.

Sarah I might well ask what was the matter with you?

Ruth There is nothing whatever the matter with me.

Norman May I put in a word for the rational man?

Ruth No, you may not. We've heard quite enough from you for one week-end.

Norman So much for the rational man.

Ruth By all means have your children. I'm not asking you to deny yourself, as you put it. All I'm saying is, for God's sake don't stand about looking martyred once you've had them. And don't look down your nose at the rest of us.

Sarah I'm not prepared to get into another argument over this, Ruth. You don't know what you're talking about. You never will.

Ruth She is so dogmatic. Reg, I feel sorry for you. How do you live with a woman like this who's so pig-headed? She just will not listen.

Sarah Listen . . .

Ruth She will not listen to a single word.

Sarah Will you listen to me for a minute. If I feel sorry for anyone, it's Norman.

Norman A blow for the rational man.

Sarah Have you ever consulted him? Of course you haven't. You've just gone selfishly ahead with your own career . . .

Ruth While you're busy manufacturing lots more little Reggies and Sarahs. What a wonderful contribution that is.

Sarah Oh well, if we're going to get personal.

Ruth If that isn't selfishness and conceit of the worst sort, I don't know what is. (*Banging down her spoon angrily*) And this is absolutely revolting, I don't know how anyone can eat it.

Ruth pushes her bowl angrily from her. It knocks Reg's wine glass and spills the contents over his trousers

Reg (*jumping up angrily*) Oh, for crying out loud.
Ruth I'm sorry. I'm sorry. Here . . . (*She flings her napkin at him*)
Reg Look at these trousers. Why the hell don't you watch what you're doing?
Sarah All right. Don't make a fuss.
Reg What?
Sarah Don't start losing your temper over a little thing like that.
Reg Now, don't you start on about people losing their tempers. If anyone's got a temper in this room, we know who that is.
Sarah I don't know how you have the nerve to say that.
Norman May I interrupt here?
Reg I'm going to change these. I'm soaking.
Sarah It wouldn't be surprising if I did have a temper living with you.
Norman Without displaying any prejudice, my wife is obviously to blame for this.
Ruth Norman, don't you start.
Norman She is the original irrational woman.
Annie Norman.
Reg I am going to change my trousers.

Reg goes out to the house

Norman She has no feelings of womanhood, let alone motherhood.
Annie Norman.
Ruth You really do ask for it, don't you?
Norman And you're jealous of those that have.
Annie Norman (*She rises*)
Ruth You just say one more thing, Norman
Norman You've got as much feeling as a dried up tea bag.
Sarah (*shrilly*) Stop it.
Annie Norman.
Tom (*rising and pushing Annie back into her seat*) Right. That's quite enough from you.
Norman Eh?
Tom I warned you, Norman.

Tom launches an unexpected blow at Norman. Norman falls off his chair

Annie Tom!
Sarah (*drumming on the table with her fists*) Stop it! Stop it! Stop it!
Tom There.
Ruth Serve you right.
Tom I warned you. I warned him, you know.
Norman What did you do that for? (*He gets up*)
Tom I did warn you. I said if you upset Annie any more. I'm afraid I can't sit by and have her called names by you.

Norman What names?

Tom Well, you called her a—tea bag or something. That is not on. I won't have that.

Norman You fool. I wasn't talking to her.

Tom What?

Norman I was talking to my wife.

Tom Oh. Were you? Oh, that's rather different.

Ruth (*rising*) Oh, thank you. Meaning I am an old tea bag, I suppose.

Tom No, I didn't mean that.

Ruth Oh, to hell with the lot of you.

Ruth storms out to the house

Norman You great idiot.

Tom I'm very sorry. I thought you were talking to Annie.

Norman You great stupid—vet.

Tom (*trying to help him*) I really am terribly . . . Can I . . . ?

Norman Oh, go away. Just go away.

Tom (*moving to go*) Yes, yes, of course. I'm sorry. (*Turning in the doorway*) Misunderstanding, you see. Oh gosh.

Tom goes out to the house

Annie Tom—oh, Norman, how could you.

Annie follows Tom out

Sarah sits in a state near to traumatic shock. She is visibly shaking. Norman rises

Norman Lunatic . . . (*He paces about*)

Sarah This is the last time I do anything for this family.

Norman Do you know he could have killed me? If I'd fallen awkwardly. If I'd fallen that way instead of this way—I'd have broken my neck. Sobering thought. But who would have cared, Sarah? Who would have cared?

Sarah How could they? How could they do it? How could they behave like that?

Norman (*moving to Sarah*) We are misunderstood people, Sarah. Misunderstood. (*He pats her head*)

Sarah (*suddenly lunging and clinging to him*) Oh, Norman.

Norman We are definitely misunderstood.

CURTAIN

SCENE 2

The same. Monday, 8 a.m.

Annie comes in with a tray of breakfast things. She is now dressed as before in Act I, Scene 1. She starts to lay the table

Sarah comes in

Sarah Oh . . .
Annie 'Morning.
Sarah You're already doing it.
Annie Yes.
Sarah (*sitting at the table*) I was going to get breakfast.
Annie Were you?
Sarah You should have let me.
Annie It's all right.
Sarah Well, we have to be off early. We won't be needing anything very much.
Annie There isn't anything very much. Toast. Remains of the marmalade. Jam—damson, I think.
Sarah That'll do us nicely.
Annie Good. Well, it's all there. Help yourself.
Sarah I suppose I better give Reg a call.
Annie No, no, Don't over-exert yourself. I'll do it.
Sarah Thank you. He's in the sitting-room, I think. He should've brought down our suitcases.
Annie Right.

Annie goes out

Sarah selects a piece of toast, examines it, finds it a little burnt and scrapes it distastefully. She sniffs the butter, finds it more or less okay. She sniffs the rather ancient looking nearly empty jar of marmalade. This she does reject. She starts spreading her toast

Norman comes in

Norman Ah-ha. Breakfast. Good morning.
Sarah (*not very warmly*) Good morning.
Norman Sleep well? (*He changes the low chair and sits above Sarah*)
Sarah No.
Norman I did.
Sarah Good.
Norman Are you angry with me?
Sarah No.
Norman This toast going free?

Sarah Yes.

Norman Cheer up, Sarah.

Sarah And what is there to cheer me up? I have never been through such a shattering week-end in my life.

Norman I'm sorry.

Sarah It wasn't all your fault. Most of it was. But not entirely.

Norman I think you ought to take care of yourself, you know.

Sarah How do I do that?

Norman Well. We don't want to lose you, do we?

Sarah I don't think some people would mind one way or the other.

Norman You find it hard to relax. That's the problem. I know that's your problem because it's my problem. As we were saying last night—I don't know how you keep going. I mean, I don't have two children and a house to run—and a husband. I've just got me. That's bad enough.

Sarah I should imagine it would be.

Norman But two children . . .

Sarah You try explaining that to some people. Your wife, for example.

Norman Oh, well quite. She wouldn't understand.

Sarah She doesn't.

Norman I know as far as I'm concerned the whole thing's a miracle. Children. Just to think of the act of actually having them. Amazing. Damn it, Sarah, you've got something to be proud of, haven't you? If you look at it this way, just by having those kids of yours, you have been responsible for two miracles.

Sarah Well, it's not that difficult.

Norman It is to me. I've never done a miracle. I saw a film on it once. Childbirth. It came out as far as its ears and I fainted. Mind you, you wouldn't have been looking at it from that angle.

Sarah I was unconscious. Both times.

Norman Ah.

Sarah It's afterwards, looking after them.

Norman Quite.

Sarah That's when it's difficult.

Norman You must be exhausted. How old are they now?

Sarah Denise is seven and Vincent's five.

Norman Seven years you've been looking after children. Would it be impertinent to ask when you last had a holiday?

Sarah I hoped this week-end was going to be one but . . .

Norman No, be honest with me, Sarah. When did you last have a holiday?

Sarah I do not remember. It was too long ago.

Norman Exactly. (*Pause*) You ought to get away. You need to. Can't you say to Reg, Reg, I need a couple of days even. I must get away.

Sarah He wouldn't take me away. And who's going to look after the children. It's no holiday with them. It was difficult enough this week-end. I was racing round organizing things, arranging this . . .

Norman Go on your own. Leave him to look after them, for a change.

Sarah Him?

Norman Why not?

Sarah Huh! (*Pause*) I wouldn't want to go on my own. What fun is it on your own?

Pause

Norman I'll take you if you like.

Sarah I beg your pardon?

Norman I said I'll take you.

Sarah On holiday?

Norman If you'd like to go.

Sarah You must think I was born yesterday.

Norman I would.

Sarah You really have got a nerve.

Norman I only offered. All right, all right . . .

Sarah First Ruth, then Annie, then me.

Norman Oh, Annie. That was different.

Sarah How?

Norman Well, it was. This would just be a holiday. For you. I'd take you round, give you a good week-end. Wouldn't you enjoy that?

Sarah No.

Norman Somewhere nice. What about Bournemouth? Ever been to Bournemouth?

Sarah I have no desire to go to Bournemouth.

Norman I've made you the offer. I leave it to you. Think about it. It would be above board. I'd book us a nice hotel. Breakfast in bed— separate breakfast. Separate beds. Separate rooms. Can't you imagine it? We'd wake up in the morning, side by side, in our separate rooms and there's the sea. And we've got all day to look at it. No children to worry about. No husband to run after . . .

Sarah Just you.

Norman Just me. I'd like to see you happy, Sarah.

Sarah Yes?

Norman Yes. Is that wrong of me? To want to see you happy?

Sarah Depends how you do it.

Norman I'd give you a good time. We'd have fun. Have you ever been to Bournemouth? It's a great place. Laugh a minute.

Sarah I can just see us going.

Norman I'd very much like to make you happy.

Sarah Pass the jam, would you?

Norman Here.

Reg enters

Reg Ah, now where's the food? (*He sits*)

Sarah Where have you been? (*She pours a cup of tea for Reg*)

Norman passes the tea to Reg

Reg What do you mean, where have I been?

Sarah Annie was supposed to call you ages ago.

Reg She did. I popped upstairs to Mother.

Sarah What for?

Reg With the magazines. I took your magazines up to Mother. You told me to. Oh, Tom's here. Told you he'd come back, didn't I? Well, he's come back. I was looking out of the sitting-room window and there he was, lurking in the garden. I told him I thought he was a cat burglar. (*He laughs*) I'm ravenous.

Sarah Yes, all right. Well, just get yourself a piece of toast. We've got to go.

Reg What's the hurry?

Sarah Because I want to get home early.

Reg What on earth for? The children aren't due back till this afternoon.

Sarah And before that, I have to go over the house from top to bottom, don't I? You may not realize it but the house has to be cleaned. It doesn't clean itself.

Reg You cleaned it before we left. Nobody's been in it since. How can it have got dirty?

Sarah It's been standing for a whole week-end. Anyway, Mrs Bridges comes to clean tomorrow. I want to make sure it's clean before she does.

Reg Oh, I give up. (*He rises and moves to the toast-rack*)

Sarah You don't understand. You never will.

Reg Not much here to eat, is there?

Sarah That's because there's nothing in the house.

Reg You're telling me. I've been starving since Saturday morning. On a diet of lettuce and soup.

Sarah Now you know what it's like with nobody running after you, don't you?

Reg Oh, blimey, look at this toast, all cold and flabby. I can't eat this.

Sarah Well, go and make some fresh.

Reg Where?

Sarah In the greenhouse. Where do you think?

Reg All right, all right. You're in a really cheery mood this morning, aren't you?

Reg goes out, taking the toast-rack

Norman (*confidentially*) It's difficult, isn't it? I know. Difficult sometimes . . . (*He pats her hand*)

Sarah Don't do that.

Norman Why not?

Sarah Because you're covering me in jam.

Norman Sorry. (*He licks the jam off her hand*)

A pause

Sarah Were you just thinking about my health?

Norman When?

Sarah When you mentioned about this holiday? Did you want to take
me away just for my health?
Norman Well, that came into it. There might be any number of reasons.
I'm easy. (*He smiles*)
Sarah So long as I know. (*She smiles*)

Ruth enters

Ruth Norman.
Norman Hallo.
Ruth I'm ready.
Norman Right. Want a spoonful of jam? That's all there is. 'Till Reg
arrives with a blazing sliced loaf.
Ruth I can wait.
Norman Okay.
Ruth Good morning, Sarah. (*No reply*) Guess who isn't speaking to me
this morning. I'll be in the sitting-room, Norman, when you can tear
yourself away from Mother Doom here.
Norman Coming.

Ruth goes out to the house

Sarah Reg gets home about half past six in the evening on weekdays.
Norman Busy man.
Sarah If you feel like giving me a ring, any time. I'm usually tied to the
house. I don't get out much.
Norman I'd make you happy, Sarah.
Sarah Yes.
Norman 'Bye-bye.

Norman goes out to the house, eating the last of his toast

Sarah looks thoughtful. She gives a pleased grunt

Reg enters with the empty toast-rack

Reg Dear oh dear. (*He sits at the table*)
Sarah Have you got it?
Reg What?
Sarah I thought you were going to make yourself some toast.
Reg Oh, I don't know. I looked at the grill and I looked at the loaf and
I thought—that's a lot of effort for a piece of toast. I'll make do with
this piece.
Sarah Well, I've finished.
Reg Tea's cold as well now. Not my day, is it?
Sarah No, I don't think it is.

Annie and Tom enter from the house

Annie Look who's here.
Reg I told you he was here.
Tom 'Morning. 'Morning, Sarah.
Sarah Hallo, Tom. Bright and early.
Tom Yes. I didn't sleep very well, I'm afraid.
Annie Just tea, Tom?
Tom Just a cup, thank you.
Reg It's stone cold.
Annie Well, I'll hot it up. That's easy enough.

Annie goes out with the teapot

Tom I wanted to apologize for last night.
Sarah What?
Tom Well—lashing out—Norman. Totally lost control. Feel very embarrassed about it.
Sarah Nobody hurt fortunately.
Tom No, I didn't get a very good swing. Bit rusty.
Sarah Just as well.
Tom Yes. Rather.
Sarah I'm glad you've come back, anyway.
Tom I'm afraid I don't seem to be able to keep away.
Sarah It'll be nice for Annie with us all going.
Tom I'm only here for a second. I'm actually on my way to a call. Horse. Fetlock.
Sarah Oh.
Tom Not too serious. She can wait.
Reg Let her stand on three legs for a bit. (*He laughs*)
Tom No, she can stand all right.
Sarah Well, I hope you'll look after Annie for us.
Tom Oh, yes, I'll do my best. I think she really looks after me. (*He laughs*).
Sarah Yes, well, you mustn't let it get too one-sided, must you?
Tom What? Oh. No. I do help . . .
Sarah Yes. It depends what you do though, doesn't it?
Tom I did the ceiling in the kitchen. And . . .
Sarah No, I meant a little more than that.
Reg I thought we were in a hurry.
Sarah Oh. Yes.
Reg Will we see you at Christmas, Tom? Or are you going to Scotland again?
Tom Probably.
Reg Oh, well. Sometime. All the best.

Annie enters with the teapot

Annie Are you off?
Sarah Yes, we must. (*She rises*)
Annie Okay. I'll come and see you've got everything. Here you are, Tom I topped it up. (*She puts the pot on the table*)

Tom Thanks.
Annie Be back in a sec.
Reg 'Bye.
Sarah Good-bye, Tom.
Tom 'Bye.

Sarah, Annie and Reg go out

Tom sits alone. He puts a plate in front of himself, then sees the empty toast-rack. He pours the tea. It is practically white

Tom Oh. Oh well . . . (*He sits and sings to himself. Tom, on his own, is amazingly cheerful. He amuses himself by arranging the things on the table in a strange secret pattern of his own*)

At length, Annie returns

Annie All right? (*She sits at the table*)
Tom Fine. All gone have they?
Annie Just about. Norman and Ruth seem to be having trouble starting their car.
Tom Oh, should I . . . (*He half rises*)
Annie No. Enjoy your tea.
Tom Oh, yes.
Annie Have you got any tea in there or is it just milk?
Tom No, it is tea. Bit anaemic.
Annie I'll make some more in a minute. Quite a week-end.
Tom Yes.
Annie I've behaved very badly. I'm sorry.
Tom No. It's me . . .
Annie No. (*Pause*) Tom . . .
Tom Um?
Annie Has your—opinion of me gone down as a result of this week-end? I mean, do you think less of me?
Tom Good Lord, no.
Annie You still—like me?
Tom Oh, yes. Of course I do.
Annie You'll still come round?
Tom You bet. (*He laughs*) Once you've improved the tea, anyway.
Annie The only reason I said I would go with Norman, you see, was—I suddenly felt very lonely.
Tom Yes, I understand. It's all right. We all get lonely. If you're lonely again and I'm not here, why don't you give me a ring?
Annie (*picking up a dessert-spoon and twiddling it in her fingers*) This is a very big house, you see. Most of the time it's just Mother and me here. We'll have to sell it eventually, it's ridiculous.
Tom I wouldn't do that.
Annie We'll have to. We'll have to move somewhere smaller. Perhaps in Essex. Or Norfolk. Or Northumberland.

Tom Bit off the beaten track.
Annie Yes.
Tom Wouldn't see much of me.
Annie No.
Tom Well, if you do sell it, make sure you give me first refusal, won't you?
  (*He gets up*) Well, I'd better go and see to my horse.
Annie Yes. Go and see to your horse.

Annie turns the side plate in front of her upside down on the table. She bangs on it deliberately with a spoon. A regular sort of rhythm which, although not fast, grows in intensity until the plate breaks

Tom (*watching her curiously*) What on earth are you doing?
Annie Breaking things. Breaking things for breakfast.
Tom (*laughs awkwardly*) Careful of splinters.

  Norman rushes in, in his coat and hat

Norman Disaster! We cannot start it.
Tom Oh goodness. Want a hand?
Norman Need one of these ex-boxers to give it a shove.
Tom Right. My pleasure. Probably see you later, Annie.
Annie Yes.

  Tom goes to the garden

Norman is about to follow when he notices Annie and the plate

Norman What are you doing? Don't tell me, you've finally run out of food. I told you, you'd get round to eating the plates eventually. Now the nicest way to eat a plate—is spread it with a thin layer of jam and then pour custard all over the . . .

Annie flies at Norman and clings on to him

Annie Oh, Norman . . .
Norman Only you want to make sure it's thick custard.
Annie (*muffled*) I want . . .
Norman Eh?
Annie I want . . .
Norman I can't hear you. What?
Annie (*in a wail*) I want to go to East Grinstead.
Norman (*soothing her*) All right. Fine. I'll take you. I'll take you.
Annie (*tearfully*) Will you?
Norman Just say the word. Come on now, don't cry. I'll make you happy. Don't worry. I'll make you happy.

Norman hugs her to him. Annie clings on. Norman looks towards the window, then out front, smiling happily

CURTAIN

FURNITURE AND PROPERTY LIST

ACT I

SCENE 1

On stage: Large dining table. *On it:* 6 roses
4 matching dining chairs
2 easy chairs with antimacassars and cushions
China cabinet. *On it:* table lamp

Standard lamp
Plant stand and plant
Sideboard. *On top:* round tray with 6 glasses, cruet set, biscuit tin
    containing water biscuits. *In cupboard:* 4 side plates in a pile
    (Act I), 6 side plates in a pile (Act II), 6 wine glasses, 4 rush mats.
    In top drawer: 3 tray cloths, duster, 8 starched damask table napkins.
    In cutlery drawer: 6 knives, 6 forks, 6 dessert spoons. *In bottom
    drawer:* 6 place mats
Garden bench in garden
Shelves with china
Carpet

Off stage: Vase with water (**Annie**)
           Waste-paper basket (**Reg**)
           Wine glass half-full of parsnip wine (**Tom**)
           Dustpan and brush (**Annie**)
           Jar of salad cream (**Sarah**)

           Bottle of home-made carrot wine (**Tom**)
           Tray with 4 plates of salad (**Annie**)

Personal: **Annie:** handkerchief
           Sarah: handbag with handkerchief and compact
           Annie, Sarah, Reg, Tom: wrist watches

SCENE 2

Strike: Everything from table

Off stage: Tray with 4 side plates, 4 knives, toast-rack, jam, marmalade, napkin,
           butter dish, 2 jam spoons (**Sarah**)
           Tray with 4 cups, saucers and teaspoons, sugar bowl and spoon,
           large jug of milk, hot-water jug, teapot, rush mat (**Annie**)
           Packet of Puffa Puffa Rice (**Sarah**)
           Packet of cornflakes (**Sarah**)
           3 cereal bowls and spoons (**Sarah**)

Personal: **Ruth:** handbag with compact, handkerchief, car keys
           Ruth: wrist watch

ACT II

SCENE 1

Strike: Everything from table

Set: Cruet and biscuit tin on sideboard
           6 glasses on tray on sideboard

Off stage: 4 knives, 4 forks, 4 spoons (**Annie**)
           Duster (**Sarah**)

Apron (Sarah)
Odd dining chair (Reg)
Low chair (Reg)
Bottle of home-made parsnip wine and corkscrew (Sarah)
Tray with 4 plates of sparse salad (Sarah)
Saucepan with stew, ladle, with 2 tea towels round handles (Annie)
6 soup plates (Reg)

SCENE 2

Strike: Everything from table

Off stage: Tray with 6 side plates, 6 cups, 6 saucers and teaspoons, milk jug,
hot-water jug, jar of jam, jar of marmalade, rush mat, butter
dish, napkin, 6 knives, 1 dessert spoon, toast-rack, with 3 pieces
of toast, sugar bowl and spoon, teapot (Annie)
Hot water to refill teapot

LIGHTING PLOT

Property fittings required: standard lamp, table lamp, pendant (dressing only)
Interior. A dining-room. The same scene throughout

ACT I, SCENE 1. Evening
To open: Effect of early evening sunshine
No cues

ACT I, SCENE 2. Morning
To open: Effect of bright summer morning
No cues

ACT II, SCENE 1. Evening
To open: Effect of late evening light, summer
No cues

ACT II, SCENE 2. Morning
To open: As Act I, Scene 2
No cues

EFFECTS PLOT

ACT I

SCENE 1

Cue 1   **Reg:** "Hardly at all."   (Page 17)
Record off stage of Richard Tauber singing "Girls were made to Love and Kiss", continue for a few moments, then fade

Cue 2   **Sarah:** ". . . a civilized meal."   (Page 19)
Bring up record as above until Curtain falls

SCENE 2

No cues

ACT II

SCENE 1

No cues

SCENE 2

No cues

THE NORMAN CONQUESTS

LIVING TOGETHER

A Play

ALAN AYCKBOURN

SAMUEL FRENCH

LONDON
NEW YORK   TORONTO   SYDNEY   HOLLYWOOD

ISBN 0 573 01573 2

LIVING TOGETHER

First presented by the Library Theatre Co., Scarborough in June 1973 and subsequently by the Greenwich Theatre Company in May 1974, and in London by Michael Codron at the Globe Theatre in August 1974, with the following cast of characters:

Norman	Tom Courtenay
Tom	Michael Gambon
Sarah	Penelope Keith
Annie	Felicity Kendal
Reg	Mark Kingston
Ruth	Bridget Turner

The play directed by Eric Thompson
Setting by Alan Pickford

The action passes in the sitting-room of a Victorian vicarage-type house during a week-end in July

ACT I
    Scene 1   Saturday, 6.30 p.m.
    Scene 2   Saturday, 8 p.m.

ACT II
    Scene 1   Sunday, 9 p.m.
    Scene 2   Monday, 8 a.m.

Period – the present

ACT I

Scene 1

The sitting-room. Saturday, 6.30 p.m.

It is a high-ceilinged Victorian room in need of redecoration. A french window leads to the garden, and a door to the rest of the house. Furnishings include a settee, easy chair, pouffe, a small table, a coffee-table, and a fireplace in front of which is a brown fur rug

As the Curtain *rises, Sarah, in a light summer coat and dress, is in the process of lifting a suitcase from the floor on to the table to open it. Reg enters from the garden in cap and sports jacket, carrying another bag and a large pile of magazines tied with string. He is followed by Norman, bearded in woolly hat and raincoat, carrying his own battered suitcase. Norman flings himself into the easy chair and sits grumpily. Reg puts the magazines on the table behind the settee*

Reg That's the lot. Well, come on. Where is she then? Where is she? Where's my little sister?

Sarah Ssh. Mother's resting.

Reg Oh. (*Wandering back to the window*) We ought to cut down the vegetation in the tennis court and have a game, Norman. Fancy a game?

Norman I hate tennis.

Sarah I thought you were in a hurry to go somewhere, Norman.

Norman Not at all.

Reg Yes, I thought you said you had a—librarians' conference.

Norman It's been cancelled.

Reg When?

Norman About ten seconds ago. Due to lack of interest.

Reg Funny lot these librarians. Now, where's Annie, do you know?

Sarah She's in there.

Reg Ah. (*He moves to the door*)

Sarah Wait.

Reg Why?

Sarah She's busy. Tom's in there with her, having a talk.

Reg Well, she can talk to Tom any time. I've come all the way to see her.

Sarah Wait.

Reg What made her change her mind? About going? I mean, I thought the idea was, we came down here, nursed Mother for the week-end and Annie went off somewhere and had a good time. No point in us being here now, is there? Might as well not have come. Not that I mind. Nice to see the country. Beautiful evening. No kids . . .

Sarah Where did you pack that present for Mother?

Reg What present?

Sarah The bed-jacket. The blue bed-jacket, it was wrapped in tissue. Where is it?

Reg Never set eyes on it.

Sarah (*removing a large playing board, bits of cardboard, etc. from the case*) What's all this you've packed?

Reg My game.

Sarah Why did you want to bring it down here?

Reg I thought there might be someone around, we could try it out. I've invented it, I want to try it out. I mean, the kids won't play it with me, you won't play it with me—how do I know if it works if no-one'll play it? Norman can play.

Norman Eh?

Sarah I should think Norman's had enough of games, haven't you, Norman?

Reg Eh?

Sarah Anyway, Norman's going in a minute, aren't you, Norman?

Reg What's all this? What's going on between you two?

Sarah I'll tell you later.

Reg (*putting the game on the coffee-table*) Oh, yes . . . ? If you're planning an affair, let me know and I'll book my holiday.

Sarah (*giving up her search*) Oh well, that's that. No present for Mother. You've forgotten to pack it. Oh well, I'll give her these magazines and tell her we'll send the bed-jacket on to her. It took me ages to make that. If you knew how I hated knitting.

Reg We do. We know. We sat round all winter watching her with bated breath. One dropped stitch and you could say good-bye to your supper . . . Hey, one of my little men is missing.

Sarah Oh, my God.

Reg I've lost my Chief Superintendent. Is he at the bottom of the suitcase? (*He goes to look in the suitcase*)

Sarah I have no idea. Our house is littered with little men.

Reg And she's complaining. (*He chuckles*)

Sarah You're very pensive, Norman.

Norman I'm wondering which is the cleanest and quickest way to finish myself off.

Reg Well, don't get married. That's long and messy. Ah-ha, here he is. (*He holds up a small cardboard figure on a base which he has rescued from the suitcase*) The Chief Superintendent in person. Nearly had a nasty accident. Got himself tangled up in a nasty web of blue woolly . . . oh.

Sarah Give that to me. (*She retrieves her bed-jacket from Reg*)

Reg (*putting the figure with the game*) It was there all the time. Just needed a good copper to find it.

Sarah Would you mind taking these upstairs.

Reg (*taking the suitcases*) My pleasure. (*He moves to the door whistling*)

Sarah And don't wake Mother if she's dozing.

Reg I'll go and say hallo to Annie first.

Sarah I've told you, she's . . .

Reg I haven't seen her for three months. She's my sister. I want to say hallo.

Sarah She and Tom are . . .

Reg Oh, to blazes with Tom.

Reg goes out to the house, whistling

Sarah (*turning her attention to Norman*) It's no good sitting there looking sorry for yourself. I'm appalled at you, I really am.

Norman (*jeering*) Jealous?

Sarah Don't be disgusting. Annie of all people. How could you? What on earth made you do it?

Norman I haven't done anything.

Sarah Annie has told me everything.

Norman Has she? And what could she possibly tell you?

Sarah About you two—last Christmas. In this house. With your wife ill upstairs—rolling about with her sister on this very rug.

Norman Oh—that—that was just festive fun.

Sarah And if that isn't enough, planning to sneak off with her for some sordid week-end.

Norman There's nothing sordid about East Grinstead. She wanted to come. I wanted to go. Don't you see? It would have been something different for her—exciting. And for me. She's stuck here, all on her own, day after day looking after that old sabre-toothed bat upstairs . . .

Sarah Will you not refer to Mother like that.

Norman Oh, come on. She's not your mother, she's not my mother. She's a mother-in-law. Fair game. I'll call her what I like. You ought to hear what Annie calls her sometimes. Anyway, we happen to love each other. Me and Annie, that is, not me and mother-in-law.

Sarah Don't be ridiculous. You're married to Ruth.

Norman What's that got to do with it?

Sarah And Annie, I may remind you, has her fiancé to consider.

Norman (*scornfully*) Her who?

Sarah Her—well—her whatever she calls him—Tom.

Norman Tom.

Sarah Yes. He may not be ideal in many ways but beggars can't be choosers . . .

Norman She's not a beggar.

Sarah Maybe not. But it would be stupid to make out she had a very wide choice as regards a possible husband. She's not—well . . .

Norman She's beautiful.

Sarah I'm not going to argue. Certainly no-one could describe her as beautiful. I'll admit she has a great deal of . . .

Norman Anybody I love is automatically beautiful.

Sarah Oh, Norman, don't be ridiculous.

Norman Have you never felt that way? Perhaps you've never been in love. Maybe that's your trouble. Was Reg never beautiful in your eyes?

Sarah I'm not discussing my private life . . .

Norman You're being free enough with mine, aren't you?

Sarah Yours doesn't happen to be particularly private, does it? It happens
to involve about half a dozen people. You, Annie, Ruth, Tom, Reg, me
and Mother.

Norman I've never asked Mother for a week-end anywhere. (*Moving to the
window*) Look at that cat up there. He's still up that tree. Tom was trying
to get it down. He can't be much of a vet. What sort of a vet are you,
when you terrify your patients into climbing trees? Something wrong
with his basket-side manner, I'd say. What do you say, Sarah? Would
you say you were a fulfilled person?

Sarah I don't know what you mean.

Norman Are you happy then?

Sarah Yes—mostly. Occasionally. Now and then. I don't know. I don't
have time to think about it. When you've a family like mine you're too
busy . . .

Norman You're very lucky. I can't say Ruth and I are happy.

Sarah Well, I'm not surprised if you . . . (*Checking herself*) She's not the
easiest person I admit.

Norman No.

Sarah Then neither are you.

Norman I'm very warm and affectionate, you know.

Sarah Yes. So are dogs. But they don't make particularly good husbands.

Norman Ah well, like me, they invariably marry—lady dogs. Perhaps I
should leave her.

Sarah Yes, do. Please do. I think it would be better for both of you. But
for heaven's sake, clear off completely and whatever you do, stop
pestering Annie. She doesn't want you, not really.

Norman I supposed you talked her out of going away with me.

Sarah I didn't need to. She'd already made up her own mind. I certainly
didn't encourage her . . . I must go up and see Mother.

Norman It was going to be a lovely time. We were going to meet behind
the post office in the village at seven o'clock and steal away on the bus
to our hotel. Forget everything, everybody, just lie anonymously in each
other's arms. Just for a day.

Sarah We'd still be here when you came back.

Norman I feel terribly depressed.

Sarah Serve you right.

Norman You haven't told Tom, have you?

Sarah That's up to Annie. Nothing to do with me.

Norman Nothing? You only talked her out of going.

Sarah I have already said, I did no such thing. It was Annie's decision.

Norman I hope she doesn't tell Tom.

Sarah Why?

Norman It'd upset him.

Sarah It's a bit late to consider his feelings now, isn't it? Having tried to
steal Annie from under his nose.

Norman I wasn't stealing her, I was borrowing her. For the week-end.

Sarah Make her sound like one of your library books.

Norman She was borrowing me, too. It was mutual. It was a friendly loan. We never intended to upset anybody. We both agreed. That was the joy of it, don't you see? Nobody need ever have known. If Annie hadn't gone and told you—nobody.

Sarah Oh, well. It's up to Annie if she wants to tell Tom. Nothing to do with me. (*She tries to lift the magazine pile*) Oh, these are far too heavy, I'll get Reg to take them up later. Now, for goodness' sake, Norman, pull yourself together and go home to Ruth.

Norman Why did you stop her going, Sarah? Be honest. Why?

Sarah I've told you why . . .

Sarah goes out to the house with the bed-jacket

Norman (*mournfully*) I really am very depressed. (*He mooches about. He pulls a magazine from the pile and flips through it. Something catches his eye and he starts reading. After a moment, he starts to laugh. He finds the article increasingly hysterical*)

Annie comes in. She stares at him

Annie Norman. (*She closes the door*)

Norman (*springing up guiltily*) Oh. Hallo, Annie.

Annie You all right?

Norman Yes, I was just trying to cheer myself up.

Annie Looks like you've succeeded.

Norman No.

Annie Norman, I'm awfully sorry. Really. I expect Sarah's told you.

Norman She said you'd thought better of it.

Annie Yes. I feel dreadful after all the trouble you've taken. Booking East Grinstead and things. It's just . . .

Norman It's all right. (*Pause*) Oh, why did you let her talk you out of it.

Annie I didn't.

Norman Don't tell me you'd have changed your mind if she hadn't . . .

Annie Things were getting very complicated, you see. I mean, when we were planning it, last Christmas and on the phone and things—well—it was simple then, wasn't it? It was easy just to forget about Ruth and —Tom and so on. Not that Tom's all that important but after all, you are married to Ruth and she is my sister, even if I'm not all that fond of her, but I don't think I'm very good at pretending for very long. Sarah got it out of me in no time.

Norman Yes. She would.

Annie And I don't think I'd have been much fun to be with, anyway. I'd have been worrying all the time. Are you furious with me?

Norman No.

Annie Oh, Norman, you look so miserable. (*Kneeling on the rug*) I am sorry.

Norman Don't . . .

Annie What?

Norman Don't kneel on that rug if you don't mind. It reminds me.

Annie Oh, yes. Our rug. (*She gives a short giggle*) I got the fire-tongs mended.

Norman Oh, yes.

Annie Tom fixed them.

Norman Oh. What does he have to say about all this?

Annie Tom? I don't think he knows.

Norman He doesn't?

Annie I haven't told him.

Norman Oh.

Annie Sarah might.

Norman I bet she will. She said she won't. But she will. She'll be dropping big circular hints. She's never kept a secret in her life . . .

Annie She'll have to chalk it up in huge letters. You know, I'm really very fond of Tom but he really is terribly heavy going: Like running uphill in roller skates. Not like you. "Beautiful sunset, isn't it, Tom?" "Um." Everything's um. Probably works a treat when he's stamping out swine fever, but it's pretty boring over dinner. "Do you like the wine, Tom?" "Um." Honestly, Norman?

Norman Mmm? I mean, yes.

Annie What are you going to tell Ruth?

Norman What I was going to tell her anyway. I've been on a conference.

Annie Which finished early?

Norman Something like that. We ran out of things to talk about. What does it matter. She won't care. She probably thinks I'm in the attic mending the roof.

Annie I didn't know assistant librarians had conferences.

Norman Everybody has conferences.

Annie You'll be able to get back all right?

Norman Yes.

Annie Oh dear . . .

Norman What?

Annie You look so limp. Like an old tea towel.

Annie impulsively leans forward to kiss him on the cheek

Reg enters

Annie jumps away and straightens the corner of the rug

Reg (*standing awkwardly*) Er—hallo again. Excuse me, just came in for something. (*He stands uncertainly*)

Norman What?

Reg What? Yes—what? Er . . . (*He picks up the waste-paper basket from behind the settee table*) Ah. This is it. This is it. Thank you. Carry on.

Reg goes out

Norman Do you ever get the feeling you're being watched? Sarah's secret agent. Our days together are numbered.

Annie So are our minutes.

Norman (*rising and going to the window*) Come on then.

Annie What?

Norman It's now or never. What do you say?

Annie What is?

Norman We can be through the gap in the hedge and half-way down the lane before they realize we've gone.

Annie (*drawing back*) Oh, Norman . . .

Norman What's to stop us? I love you—you love me—we're in love. We should be together. It's right. Believe me, it's right. We have right on our side.

Annie (*doubtfully*) Well . . .

Norman Don't you see, we're not alone? We've got the whole tradition of history behind us. We're not the first lovers who've ever done this— stood up to the whole establishment and said to hell with the *status quo*, we don't care what's meant to be, we mean this to be. Us. And there's nothing can stand in our way, you know. Not if you think about it. What is there to stop us?

Annie Mother's pills . . .

Norman Eh?

Annie I can't just rush away. I have to explain to them about Mother's pills.

Norman (*passionately*) My God! The course of true love shattered not by the furies, not by the fates but by Mother's bleeding pills.

Annie Not only that.

Norman It's all right. That's enough to be getting on with. Don't swamp me with any more overwhelming arguments. Dear Juliet, my shoelace has come undone, I cannot join you in the tomb. Love, Romeo. Dear Tristan, owing to a sudden tax demand . . .

Annie All right, Norman, all right.

Pause. Norman simmers down

Norman That's it then.

Annie Yes. That's it.

Norman Oh.

A pause

Tom enters from the house

Tom Ah.

Norman Gone. All gone.

Tom Glad I've caught you.

Norman Oh, it's Tom. Hallo, Tom. (*He shakes Tom's hand*) Haven't seen you for ages. How are you?

Tom Fine. Just been talking to you in the garden, haven't I?

Norman Oh, yes. I forgot. I think it was me.
Tom Don't quite follow you.
Norman It was probably me. On the other hand it could have been you.
Tom Me what?
Norman Talking to yourself.
Annie Norman . . .
Tom Hang on, I'm getting confused here.
Norman How unusual.
Annie Norman . . .
Norman Anyway, my mistake.
Tom (*doubtful*) Yes. I—wanted a word with you.
Annie (*moving to the door*) I'll get on out there.
Tom No. Hang on. Hang on a second, Annie. Would you mind.

Annie sits on the settee

Norman Recriminations. Here they come. (*He sits in the easy chair*)
Tom Um?
Norman Nothing.
Tom The point is . . . (*He pauses uncertainly and wanders to the window*) Is that cat still up that tree, by the way?
Norman Hanging on grimly. As we all are.
Tom I suppose he'll come down eventually . . . The point is, something seems to be going on which I've not been let into.
Norman Has it?
Tom Apparently. Sarah was talking about something.
Norman (*to Annie*) What did I tell you?
Tom What?
Norman Come on, let's have it. What did she say?
Tom That's it, you see. I couldn't make it out.
Norman You couldn't?
Tom Not really.
Norman Oh—good.
Annie Would you both like something to drink?
Tom Thought perhaps you could enlighten me.
Norman Yes, please. A great deal.
Annie I'll see what we've got.

Annie goes out

Tom Annie's a bit angry with me.
Norman Is she?
Tom Yes. You know she was planning to go away this week-end?
Norman Yes.
Tom Well, reading between the lines, I think she was rather hoping that old you-know-who would go with her.
Norman Who?
Tom Me.
Norman You?

Tom Yes.

Norman She asked you?

Tom Very obliquely.

Norman Must have been.

Tom Now she's not going. And it seems to be my fault.

Norman It is.

Tom You think so?

Norman Definitely. If she's not going away, it's entirely due to you.

Tom Yes, I was afraid of that. The question is, how do I get myself out of the dog's kennel and back in the pantry.

Norman I beg your pardon?

Tom Back in her good books.

Norman Very difficult.

Tom Is it?

Norman Want my opinion?

Tom I'd welcome it.

Norman I think you've given her too much. I think she's in danger of being spoilt. She's taking you for granted.

Tom Really?

Norman She's taking everyone for granted. What she needs is a bit of the old boot.

Tom Boot?

Norman Bit of the rough stuff.

Tom Oh, come on. Boot? Come on . . .

Norman Metaphorical.

Tom Oh, metaphorical boot. What's that exactly?

Norman Tell her she's damned lucky to have you around. And the next time she's planning holidays for two, she can come and ask you politely if you'd like to come. If you don't watch it, she'll walk all over you. Couple of sharp words, she'll jump. Tell her she looks a mess. If she wants to be seen around with you in future, she'd better smarten up her ideas. She looks like something that's fallen off a post van. I mean, what the hell right has she to promise something and then let you down at the last minute? It would serve her right if you belted her one and gave her rabies. That's my opinion. (*He pauses breathless*)

Tom (*very bewildered*) Is it?

Norman She'd respect you for that.

Tom Well, I'll bear it in mind but . . .

Annie enters with three wineglasses, three bottles of wine tucked under her arms, and a corkscrew. She is having difficulty

Annie It'll have to be the home-made stuff.

Tom (*leaping up*) Oh, let me . . . (*He takes a bottle which appears to be slipping from under her arm*)

Annie Thanks.

Tom catches Norman's eye. Norman shakes his head disapprovingly. Tom stares at the bottle he is holding. Annie stands waiting for Tom to take the other bottles from her. Instead, Tom puts his bottle back in her arms and sits on the settee

Oh, thank you so much. That's a great help. Don't put yourselves out, will you.

Norman No.

Tom No.

Annie (*putting the things on the settee table*) What's got into you two?

Norman Nothing.

Tom No.

Annie Well, if you want a drink, you can damn well open them. (*She sits on the settee*)

Tom hesitates and finally gets up. Norman clucks disapprovingly

Tom Well—parsnip or dandelion?

Norman We have a choice?

Tom Both last year's. I think I'd recommend the parsnip. It's slightly mellower. The dandelion's rather lethal. Oh, and there's some carrot.

Annie Don't touch the dandelion—it's a killer. I didn't mean to bring it in.

Tom Parsnip then?

Norman Dandelion.

Tom You sure?

Norman Positive.

Tom Oh well . . . (*He starts to open the bottles*)

Annie I have a feeling there's trouble brewing in the dining-room. I passed the door just now and Reg and Sarah seemed to be limbering up.

Norman That should set the seal on the week-end.

Annie As long as Mother doesn't hear them.

Tom No, we don't want her upset.

Annie It won't upset her. She'll insist on being carried downstairs to be in at the kill. There's nothing she likes better than a good row.

Norman In the old days she used to start them all.

Annie She and Sarah. She really loathed Sarah.

Norman Even Mother-in-law has her good side.

Annie Tom's frightened to go up there, aren't you?

Tom Well . . .

Annie She thinks he's a doctor.

Tom Can't get it through to her I'm a vet. She insists I take her pulse, listen to her—chest and other things. Very embarrassing.

Norman She's mad for the feel of manly hands. She knows what she's doing, don't worry.

Tom Yes, I think she does. (*Examining a glassful of wine*) Better just try this first. (*He samples it*)

Annie (*loudly in Norman's direction*) What's it like, Tom?

Tom Um . . . (*He ponders*)

Annie (*raising her eyebrows to heaven, softly*) Um . . .

Tom (*bringing a glass to Annie*) Not bad, not bad, here—parsnip.

Annie Thanks.

Tom (*to Norman*) Dandelion.

Norman Ta.

Annie (*examining her glass*) It's clearer than usual.

Tom Yes.

Annie It's usually like soup. You have to filter it through your front teeth.

Norman (*raising his glass by way of a toast*) Well. Um . . .

Annie (*giggling*) Um . . .

Tom Yes. Cheers. (*Pause*) Um—you know, I've been thinking. (*He sits on the settee*) What would have been rather nice. Too late now—but another year. Supposing there is another year that is . . .

Norman Why? Are you planning to bring the world to an end shortly?

Tom No, no.

Norman This is very potent.

Annie Very. Brewed by Mother. Last thing she did before she was ill.

Norman She knows her spells.

Tom What would have been rather nice . . .

Norman (*finding a bit in his glass*) Ah.

Annie What is it?

Norman Bit of cork. Or a toad's leg.

Tom What would have been awfully nice is if we'd all three gone. Don't you think.

Annie and Norman stare at him

I mean, we all get on well. It would have been rather fun . . .

Norman I beg your pardon?

Tom If Annie and you and I had all gone way together on her week-end.

Norman (*highly amused*) Oh, my God. (*Rising and crossing to the wine*) More wine . . .

Tom Single rooms, of course.

Norman (*taking up the bottle of dandelion wine and returning to his chair*) Oh, yes, single rooms.

Tom I didn't mean anything like that.

Norman (*laughing openly*) No. Nothing like that.

Tom What's funny?

Norman (*helplessly*) Nothing.

Annie (*angry*) Oh, Tom, honestly.

Tom Eh?

Annie You're so dim. You're so completely and utterly dismally dim.

Tom What?

Annie You make me mad, you're so stupid. You're boring, slow-witted, dull and utterly stupid.

Tom (*slightly injured, no more*) What have I said now? What have I said now?

Norman Now's the time to knock her down.

Annie I'm fed up with both of you. You've ruined my week-end.

Tom All I said was . . .

Annie (*yelling*) I heard what you said. Thank you very much. I heard what you said.

Norman is still laughing, highly amused by this

And, Norman, just shut up.

Norman does so. A silence

Tom Well . . .

Annie (*muttering*) Stupid men . . .

A crash and a scream from Sarah is heard from the dining-room

Norman Meanwhile, in the dining-room, the first shots are being fired in anger.

Annie (*leaping up*) Oh, no . . . (*Hurrying to the door*) I wish you'd all go away, all of you, and leave me in peace.

Annie goes out leaving her glass on the table

Tom She's like a tiger when she's roused, isn't she?

Norman I've never met a tiger socially, I wouldn't know.

Tom Something's got into her, you know. I think that holiday meant more to her than she's letting on.

Norman Yes, I'm beginning to think that. (*Proffering the bottle*) *Plus de vin?*

Tom No, no. Spoil my dinner. You'd better be careful or you'll finish up here for the night.

Norman That's a point. (*He pours himself another*)

Tom moves to the window

Tom (*calling*) Pussy, pussy. Down, puss. Come down, puss. Pussy, pussy. I wish they'd given the animal a name. I really do.

Norman pours another glass

I should go easy on that. I had a very unpleasant side reaction.

Norman It doesn't show.

Tom Well, I think I'll go and see if I can pour oil on things. Not going immediately, are you?

Norman Not immediately.

Tom Right.

Tom goes out

Norman rises to his feet and finds already he is a bit unsteady. He goes to the window

Norman (*French pronunciation*) Dan-de-lion. (*At the window; calling*) You stay up there, mate. If you come down, he'll only want paying.

Tom returns with his glass

Tom Oh, Lord . . .

Norman Back again?

Tom I think I'll keep out of there for a second. The room's positively knee. deep in home truths—if you know what I mean.

Norman Splendid.

Tom That and biscuits.

Norman Biscuits?

Tom Yes, they seem to have been throwing biscuits around. Water biscuits.

Norman You can do someone a nasty injury with a water biscuit . . .

Annie appears fleetingly in the doorway with a dustpan and brush

Annie All hell's been let loose in there.

Annie goes

Tom Do you need a . . . (*He realizes she has gone*)

Pause. Tom wanders to the table and discovers Reg's game

Tom (*examining it*) What's all this? Looks like another of Reg's home-made games. Looks even more complicated than usual. I better keep out of the way if he decides to play it. Reg gets rather irritated with me. Always very slow on getting the hang of the rules. (*Slight pause*) Norman. Frankly—answer me something.

Norman Mmm?

Tom Do you think I'm dim and dismal? I think that's what she said. Yes, that was it. Dim and dismal and stupid. Do I come across as that?

Norman Um—no. I'd say—you had the good fortune to be born without a single suspicious or malicious thought in your head.

Tom Oh, I don't know.

Norman Yes. Yes, true. And that can get you in a lot of trouble. Because you're more or less on your own, you see. And whenever people feel like taking a really good swing at something, to relieve their feelings, you come in extremely handy. No come back, you see.

Tom I haven't noticed people doing that. You've got the wrong chap.

Norman (*waving a fist in the air*) You've got to develop a come-back. (*Studying Tom*) I mean, looking at you standing there, I don't think there's anyone in there at all. You're somewhere else. That's remote control, all that lot.

Tom That stuff's beginning to tell. I warned you about the dandelion.

Norman Don't worry about a thing.

Tom Well, I'd better go and see if the dining-room's cooled off a bit. I'll take them in a bottle. (*He takes one*)

Norman Want a tip?

Tom What?

Norman Go in there laughing.

Tom Laughing?

Norman There's nothing they like better in this family than a good laugh.
Go on. Bring an atmosphere of merriment into the room. (*He gives
a false laugh*)

Tom (*copying Norman*) All right. I'll try it. You're a good chap, Norman,
you know. A very good chap.

Norman Thank you.

Tom I'm sorry you're having to dash away. To your—conference. Pity
you're not staying. You brighten the place up a bit. Pity. Cheerio.

Norman Cheerio.

Tom goes out

Norman laughs

Tom appears at the door, laughs, and goes

*Norman goes to the door and laughs. Tom is heard laughing, off. Norman
closes the door, laughing. He finds the gramophone under the occasional table,
puts it on the table, opens it, takes the record off the turntable and reads the
label, hums a line from "Girls were made to Love and Kiss". He replaces the
record. Winds the gramophone up, and starts the record. He does a dance to
the music and sings as the vocal starts. At one point he opens the door and
"sings out" to the corridor. He returns, singing, puts his glass on the floor
below the rug, and finally collapses on the rug*

Here's to you, Tom, old boy. Here's to the lot of you.

He sings louder, as—

the Curtain *falls*

Scene 2

The same. Saturday, 8 p.m.

*Norman is asleep, on the rug, with bottles and a glass beside him. Reg and
Tom enter from the house without seeing him*

Reg . . . no, no. You say to me, who's there, you see . . .

Tom Oh, it's me who says that. I see. All right. Who's there?

Reg Start again. Knock knock.

Tom Come in—I mean, who's there?

Reg Vet.

Tom Vet?

Reg No. You say, vet who?

Tom Vet who, sorry. Come in—who's there—vet who.

Reg There's no "come in". Start again.

Tom Right-ho. Knock knock.

Reg Who's there—no. I should have started it. Knock knock.
Tom Who's there?
Reg Vet.
Tom Vet who?
Reg Vet kind of door is this, you can't afford a bell. (*He laughs*)
Tom Yes, I think I've got it now—try it again.
Reg That's it.
Tom Oh, is it? Quite simple, really.
Reg Yes . . . (*Seeing Norman*) Good God! Look at that.
Tom Oh. It's Norman. (*They move to him*) Is he all right?
Reg Norman! Norman! (*No response*) He's out like a light.
Tom I thought he'd gone.
Reg So did everybody. When he finally stopped singing and peace
    descended over the fruit and cream, I thought we'd lost him. Sarah's
    going to be pleased.
Tom Ought we to move him?
Reg Well, he's not in anybody's way. Oy . . . (*He kicks Norman*)

Norman grunts

(*Moving away*) Leave him, I think. Oh, I'm starving after that meal. Salad.
    I can't bear salad. It grows while you're eating it, you know. Have you
    noticed. You start one side of your plate and by the time you've got to
    the other, there's a fresh crop of lettuce taken root and sprouted up.
    You have to start again. And it still doesn't fill you. You finish up
    exhausted and hungry. The only thing that keeps me going when I'm
    eating a salad is the hope that somebody might have thought it was my
    birthday and hidden something to eat under all the vegetation. But they
    never do. A sardine if you're lucky.
Tom (*still with Norman*) He's still breathing.
Reg I should hope so. He's enough trouble as he is without dying on us.
    The problem with this house is there's no television.
Tom It's very shallow breathing. Do you think I should take his hat off?
Reg He doesn't breathe through the top of his head, does he? Oh I don't
    know, he might do knowing Norman. (*Bending over him*) If I were you,
    I'd pull it down over his face—like this. (*He does so*) There you are, great
    improvement.
Tom It's the dandelion, you see. Look at that, he's had nearly a bottle.
    Drowning his sorrows, I suspect.
Reg Sorrows?
Tom Well, I was talking to him earlier. He was obviously very disturbed.
    Depressed . . .
Reg Was he? Well . . .
Tom Don't know why, I'm sure. You know something, though, I've got
    a theory there's probably a woman at the back of it. Man gets drunk
    like this, it's generally a woman. Ruth, do you think?
Reg Possibly. Possibly . . .
Tom Perhaps Sarah would know. She usually keeps her ear close to the
    ground. Better ask her.

Reg (*hastily*) No, I wouldn't Tom, really.

Tom No?

Reg No. The point is, Sarah did whisper something to me, as a matter of fact. Norman mentioned something to her. Confidentially.

Tom Oh. Did he? Anything we can do to help? I mean, he's a good chap. Pity to see him like this.

Reg Well apparently, he had something lined up for tonight, you see.

Tom Yes, his Annual Librarians' Conference. He told me. He'll have missed that now, won't he?

Reg No, it was something else, you see. He'd apparently lined up a bit on the side.

Tim A bit on the side?

Reg Oh, you know Norman. Any pretty girl—he's away.

Tom Oh, I see. And she's let him down?

Reg Apparently.

Tom I see. Any idea who she is?

Reg No. No. None at all.

Tom Oh. Pity. I mean, it might have been worth almost trying to contact her. Seeing if we couldn't patch things up. Mind you, if she could see him now, she'd probably feel she'd made the right decision.

Annie comes in from the house

Annie I have never known a house where you can have a blazing row over who's going to make the coffee . . . (*Seeing Norman*) Oh, no! Norman! What's the matter with him?

Reg He's taken an overdose.

Annie An overdose? Of what? (*Trying to revive Norman*) Norman— Norman.

Tom Of dandelion wine.

Annie What?

Tom He's had too much of it, that's all.

Annie You mean, he's just drunk?

Reg Give her a prize.

Annie Norman, you idiot—get up. (*She kicks him*)

Norman (*sleepily*) Hallo.

Annie Oh, look at him, he's disgusting. Sarah'll be delighted to see him. I thought he'd gone home.

Tom No, well—actually—we were just saying, he's probably like this because of his bit on the side.

Annie Bit on the side?

Reg Yes, well, we don't want to go into all that now, Tom.

Annie What bit on the side?

Tom Oh, you know Norman. Any pretty girl. He'd got some bit on the side lined up for the week-end. She went and ditched him.

Annie Norman told you that?

Reg No.

Tom You've just said he did.

Reg Yes, well he did, but . . .

Tom Yes, he did.

Annie He did. (*Kicking Norman*) Get up, you drunken slob.

Norman (*Without waking up*) Hallo.

Reg (*sitting on the pouffe*) I wouldn't do too much of that, Annie.

Annie Wouldn't you. I would. (*She kicks him again*)

Tom Sorry. I didn't mean to shock you. Did I shock you, telling you that?

Annie Yes.

Tom Oh. Sorry. Anyway, that's why he's drunk. He's been let down by . . .

Annie By his bit on the side? Well, lucky him.

Tom wanders to the window. Annie glares at Reg who whistles nonchalantly. Annie wanders to sit, passing Reg who moves his leg out of her way as she passes

Tom He's still up there. The cat. Think he's staging some sort of protest.

Annie Oh, forget the damn cat.

Tom Think I'll switch on the outside lights, if you don't mind. Might encourage him down, when it gets dark.

Tom goes out to the garden for a second, and an exterior light comes on

Reg Sarah making the coffee, is she?

Annie She was fighting for the privilege. Literally.

Tom returns

Tom Lovely evening. Going to be quite a sunset. Really quite something. You know, I don't think I altogether got the point of that vet joke.

Reg Never mind, never mind.

Annie You haven't been telling him jokes again?

Reg I tried my best.

Annie You never learn, do you? And no more rows between you and Sarah, please.

Reg I didn't so anything. Just standing there, she flung this tin of biscuits at me—oh, don't talk about biscuits, I'm starving. (*He takes two magazines from the pile*)

Annie She probably had good cause.

Reg Nonsense.

Annie Must remember to give Mother her medicine in fifteen minutes.

Tom It's on a night like this, you know, one could really fancy going out and sleeping under the stars. Used to do that when I was at college.

Reg Didn't it have a roof then? (*He sits in the easy chair with his magazines*)

Tom Yes. I meant, in the vacations. I used to take my tent and bicycle off somewhere.

Reg Yes, great that. Get a group of you together . . .

Tom No, no, mostly on my own. Preferred it. I did take someone one year but we didn't really hit it off. He was very—ebullient—I think that's the word. I don't honestly think you can possibly share a small tent for any length of time with someone who's ebullient. I remember he used to lie there in his sleeping-bag, night after night, whistling under his breath. Maddening. It was no good saying anything to him because he had this frightful temper. He couldn't bear it if you criticized him. He'd take it very personally. Practically go berserk. I remember, he once threw my canvas bath on the camp fire. Just because I said something he didn't care for. So I mostly went on my own. Watched for badgers. Impossible to watch badgers with a man like that. Anyway, he failed his finals . . .

Norman snores

Annie Oh, no, we're not going to have to put up with that all evening, are we?

Tom Yes. A whole canvas washstand. On the fire. Ruined it.

Reg If she hadn't flung those biscuits at me we could have had those.

Norman snores

Annie Norman, shut up.

Sarah comes in with the tray of coffee, etc., which she puts on the settee table

Sarah Here we are. Sorry I took so long. I had to rinse the cups again. Someone who shall be nameless had put them away without . . .

Norman snores

Oh, my God, what's that?

Annie Guess who.

Sarah Oh, no, this is too much. I'm not having this. Norman, get up this minute. Norman . . .

Reg Save your breath, he can't hear you. He's bubbling over with dandelion wine.

Sarah Revolting. Well, we can't leave him there, for heaven's sake.

Reg He's all right.

Sarah He is not all right.

Reg He isn't in anybody's way. Leave him alone.

Sarah I am not sitting down to have coffee with that all over the floor.

Reg (*irritated*) Well, what are we supposed to do with him?

Annie (*swiftly*) All right. All right. We'll move him. That's enough. We'll move him. Tom . . .

Tom Um?

Annie Give me a hand.

Reg No. I'll do it. It's all right.

Reg and Tom heave Norman half up by his arms

(*To Sarah*) Now then, madam, would you like him wrapped or will you take him as he is.

Annie (*indicating the window seat*) Put him here.

Annie replaces the bottles and glass on the settee table

Sarah (*watching them deposit Norman*) Absolutely revolting behaviour.
Reg There you go . . .
Annie (*at the coffee*) What's everybody want? White or black?
Sarah No, I'll do it . . .
Annie It's all right.
Sarah No. I'm doing this . . .
Annie I'm already doing it.
Sarah You're not already doing it, I'm doing it.
Annie Oh, don't be so ridiculous, Sarah.
Sarah I'm not being ridiculous. This is your week-end to rest.
Annie Oh, forget that.
Sarah Will you please give me that coffee-pot.
Annie What's the use of . . .
Sarah Annie, will you give me that coffee-pot at once or I shall lose my
temper.
Annie (*thrusting the pot at Sarah*) Oh, go on have the damn thing then.
(*She sits sulkily on the settee*)
Sarah Thank you. (*Recovering her composure*) Now then, everyone. Black
or white?
Reg I should heat it up first. It'll be cold by now.
Sarah (*ignoring him*) Tom?
Tom Um?
Sarah Coffee?
Tom Oh, thanks very much.
Sarah Thank you, Tom. Black or white?
Tom Um? . . . (*He considers*)

A pause

Sarah Annie?
Annie No, thank you.
Sarah Oh, don't be so silly.
Annie None for me, I couldn't drink it.
Sarah Reg?
Tom Black, I think.
Sarah (*shrilly*) I'm asking Reg.
Tom Oh. Sorry.
Reg White.
Sarah Please.
Reg Please.
Sarah At last. White for Reg. Black for Tom. None for Annie.
Tom I think I'll change mine to white on second thoughts.

Sarah gives him a glare. Norman snores

Sarah Is there any way of stopping that noise? (*Holding out two cups to
Tom*) Would you mind, Tom?

Tom takes two cups, gives one to Annie. Annie takes the cup to Reg who sits on the settee. Sarah brings her cup to the settee. Tom gets up, Sarah sits down, Tom tries to, but cannot, so wanders to the settee table and puts sugar in his coffee. He takes two magazines, goes to the low chair and sits. He stirs his coffee noisily and at length. Sarah waits for him to sit before she speaks

Sarah Well now, how would we all like to spend this evening?

A silence

It's not often we're all gathered together like this. I'm sure we can——

Norman snores

—think of something.

A silence

Reg Well, I thought it might be quite fun if we were to have a go at my game, perhaps.
Sarah I'm sure nobody wants to do that.
Reg It'd be quite fun.
Sarah We don't want to waste our evening doing that.
Reg You may not but . . .
Sarah No-one does, don't be so boring.
Reg (*muttering*) I just thought if . . .
Sarah We hardly see each other at all. One of the few occasions we all manage to be together, away from that blessed television and without the children to worry about—wouldn't it be rather nice if for once we could just sit and have a pleasant civilized conversation?
Reg Civilized conversation?
Sarah Yes, why not?
Reg We couldn't have a civilized conversation if we tried. Hark at you just now. You were only pouring the coffee out, there was practically a bloody civil war.
Sarah Well, I'm not wasting my time playing your silly games and that's final.

Silence

Annie I think I'd quite enjoy a game.
Reg Ah!
Sarah What?
Annie And I'm sure Tom would. Wouldn't you, Tom?
Tom Um?
Annie You'd like to play Reg's game, wouldn't you?
Tom (*doubtfully*) Oh . . .
Sarah Of course he doesn't, do you, Tom?
Annie Of course he does, don't you, Tom?
Tom Er . . . (*Looking from woman to woman*) Well . . .
Annie Super. Come on then, Reg.
Reg (*already unpacking the board*) If you're sure you'd like to . . .
Annie Tom . . .
Tom Yes. All right. (*He gets up*)

Reg You going to play, Sarah?

Sarah Well, I suppose if it's a choice between that and sitting on my own . . .

Reg Grand. Get me a chair, Tom.

Tom brings the low chair to Reg, who sits. Tom hovers behind him. Annie pulls the pouffe towards the coffee-table, then sits on the settee. Sarah stands and watches

Sarah I'm not playing for long. I think I'll have an early night.

Reg It's all right, it's quite a quick game.

Sarah I've heard that before.

Tom That one of yours we played before was very complicated.

Reg Ah, you mean my Mountaineering one.

Tom Yes. I seem to remember I kept running out of sherpas.

Reg Ah well, you didn't buy enough sherpa cards to start with. You need the sherpas to carry your oxygen.

Tom Yes, I ran out of that as well. My whole expedition was a total write-off.

Sarah Well, let's play this game, shall we, if we're going to.

Reg Yes, right. Well, sit where you like. Sarah, you go there. And Annie —Tom.

Tom sits on the settee

Sarah (*sitting on the pouffe*) I can't sit here. The board's upside down. I can't read it.

Tom Sit here.

Annie No, she can sit here.

Reg No, it's all right, I'll turn the board round, it's very simple.

Sarah Now you can't read it.

Reg I don't need to read it, I know.

Tom I think I can read it sideways all right.

Sarah now sits opposite Reg, Annie next to Tom

Annie It looks very exciting. (*Picking up a pile of cards*) What are these?

Reg (*anxiously*) No. Don't touch anything.

Annie Sorry.

Reg I'll explain.

Sarah Well, I hope it doesn't take all night.

Reg Right now.

Sarah Don't forget Mother's medicine, will you, Annie?

Annie Five minutes yet.

Reg Right, now. This is the board.

Tom Go slowly, won't you? I'm not awfully quick on these sort of things.

Sarah Hah!

Annie You don't say.

Tom (*a bit nettled for him*) I do my best, I do my best.

Reg Well, just listen, listen carefully. This board represents the street map of a city. Each of these areas marked brown are buildings.

Tom Buildings.

Reg Now, as you see, they are all marked very clearly what they are. These are shops, you see. Greengrocers—outfitters—bank and then along here jewellers—dress shop.

Tom What's this here? Coop. What's a coop?

Reg Co-op.

Tom Oh, co-op. I see. Sorry—reading sideways, you see.

Annie Oh, Tom, for goodness' sake.

Tom All right . . . don't keep on at me, don't keep on at me, there's a good girl.

Annie Well, honestly, you're so slow!

Reg And all these grey areas are the roads.

Sarah Oh, this is far too complicated to learn in one evening.

Reg It's not complicated if you'll listen. Now the object of the game is as follows.

Sarah I mean, it takes an hour just to read the . . .

Reg (*yelling*) Listen!

Norman (*rolling off the window-seat; waking up with a jerk, loudly*) Wah! Wah!

Everyone reacts

Sarah Oh, my God.

Norman (*getting up*) I was having a terrible dream. It was a terrible dream, you've no idea.

Annie You all right, Norman?

Norman Hallo. There was this great big black shape and it was coming after me—like a cloud—only it was making this buzzing noise. (*He demonstrates with a buzzing noise*)

Reg (*over this*) We're having a game at the moment, Norman.

Norman And I was trying to run away from it. But you know how it is in a dream, your feet won't move . . .

Tom I've had that.

Reg Yes, terrible. Now, the object of the game . . .

Norman (*threshing his feet about*) You're running, running, but you're still in the same place. You know you're dreaming but you can't wake up. Terrifying. You came into it, Sarah . . .

Sarah Yes, I think you'd better lie down.

Annie You can use my bed, if you like. I'll make up the spare one later.

Norman stumbles to the window-seat and sits

Sarah No, Norman can sleep on the spare one.

Annie No, it isn't made up.

Sarah Then I'll make it up. (*She rises*)

Reg Oh, come on we're playing a game.

Tom Is this blue thing a road?

Reg No, that's a river.

Tom Ah.

Sarah Are the sheets in the linen cupboard?

Norman rises

Annie Sarah, if you don't mind, I'll deal with it.
Sarah (*going to the door*) There is no need for you to, you're supposed to be having a rest——

Norman blunders into Sarah in the doorway

—Where are you going?
Norman Phone. I've got to phone.
Annie (*indicating the phone*) Well, use this one.
Norman Oh, yes.
Sarah Who are you phoning?
Norman My wife. Ruth. I need to speak to my wife. I demand to speak to my wife . . .

Tom fiddles with the cardboard pieces

Reg Well, phone in another room, there's a good chap . . . (*Knocking Tom's hand from the board*) And don't fiddle with those . . .
Tom Sorry.
Annie (*rising*) He'll have to phone in here. The other one's in Mother's room. God, it's nearly time for her medicine.
Norman I want to speak to Ruth.
Annie (*soothingly, guiding him to the phone*) All right, Norman—here. Sit here. You can phone from here. (*She sits Norman in the easy chair*)
Norman Thank you very much.
Annie Can you manage?
Norman God bless you and keep you.
Sarah Do you think it's wise, him speaking to Ruth?
Annie No idea.
Sarah Probably upset her more than ever.
Annie (*returning to the table*) Probably. (*She sits as before*)
Reg Sarah, are you playing or not?
Sarah (*sitting*) Yes, all right, all right. Let's get it over and done with.
Reg We haven't even started. Now then, the object of the game is as follows. With four players, two of us represent the police, and two of us, the criminals.
Norman (*on the phone*) Hallo . . .
Reg Now, the aim of the criminals——
Norman Ruth? It's me . . .
Reg —is to plan a successful raid——
Norman Me. Norman. I'm at Mother's.
Reg (*with a glare at Norman*) —on any shop they choose. The aim of the police . . .
Norman Your mother's. Of course, your mother's . . .
Reg The aim of the police, obviously, is to stop them.
Norman How the hell can I be at my mother's? She's been dead for ten years . . .
Reg Norman . . .

Norman Well, don't say it in that tone.

Reg Norman . . .

Norman God, can't we even have a—excuse me a minute. (*Covering the mouthpiece, to Reg*) What's that?

Reg Could you keep it down a bit?

Norman Beg your pardon. (*He kneels on the floor and covers his head, then speaks into the phone, softly*) Yes?

Reg Thank you. The aim of the police is to stop the raid and capture the crooks red-handed . . .

Norman (*softly into the phone*) Yes, yes. I know . . .

Reg Is that clear so far?

Sarah Perfectly clear, do get on with it.

Tom Um . . .

Reg I don't think Tom's got it. You followed it so far, Tom?

Tom I think so. Police and crooks, yes. The bit that still worries me is this river. It seems to be running straight through the Co-op. Is that right?

Reg It runs underneath it. Underneath.

Tom Oh, I see. Better not shop in the basement.

Reg (*vastly irritated*) Oh, for heaven's sake . . .

Annie Oh, Tom, do shut up.

Tom (*irritably*) All right. All right . . .

Norman (*loudly, into the phone*) I said, you're a selfish bitch . . . (*As the others turn, covering mouthpiece*) Sorry—sorry. (*Into the phone, softly*) What? Yes—yes.

Sarah Come on, Reg, get on with it.

Reg I am trying to get on with it. Now. The police can spot the criminals as follows. They have three police cars—(*holding up a model car*)—which are these. Police cars can run on the roads but not in the buildings . . .

Sarah That's a relief.

Reg Look, do you mind, do you mind. The police cars can see up to twenty spaces ahead of them and up to four spaces each side. They can't see behind them and they can't see round corners.

Sarah Why can't they see behind them?

Reg Because they can't, that's why.

Tom Motto: don't drive behind a police car.

Norman (*loudly for a second*) Love? What do you know about love . . . (*With an apologetic look at the others, continuing in a lower tone*) Have you ever felt love for a single human being in your life?

Reg The police also have the Chief Superintendent. (*Holding him up*) This chap—he can see up to three spaces ahead of him and three spaces round a corner . . .

Tom Useful chap in a crisis.

Sarah Oh, this is absurd.

Reg What's absurd?

Sarah How can you have a man see three spaces ahead and three round a corner?

Reg Because he's got a very long neck. I don't know, it's a game, woman.

Sarah It's not even realistic.

Reg What's that got to do with it?

Sarah It's not much of a game if it's not even realistic.

Reg What are you talking about? Realistic? (*Leaping up*) What about chess? That's not realistic, is it? What's wrong with chess?

Sarah Oh well, chess . . .

Reg In chess, you've got horses jumping sideways. That's not realistic, is it? Have you ever seen a horse jumping sideways?

Sarah Yes. All right . . .

Reg (*leaping about*) Like this. (*Imitating a "knight's move"*) Jumping like this. Jump, jump-jump. Jump, jump-jump. That's very realistic, I must say.

Sarah You've made your point.

Annie Reg . . .

Reg And bishops walking diagonally. (*Demonstrating again*) You ever seen a bishop walking like this? Well, have you? I'm asking you, have you ever seen a flaming bishop walking like this?

Sarah Reg, will you please sit down and get on with it.

Reg (*sitting, triumphantly*) Well then.

Norman Don't you hang up on me . . . Ruth! Ruth! (*He jangles the receiver up and down*) Hallo? Hallo? What? Who's this? Mother— what are you doing on the line, get off.

Sarah Who's he talking to?

Norman Ruth! Hallo . . . Mother, will you please get off this line.

Annie (*rising*) Oh, my God. He jiggled the receiver . . .

Norman Mother!

Annie He rang the extension bell in Mother's bedroom.

Norman (*into the phone*) Look—would you shut up, both of you, for a minute and let me get a word in . . . Mother, if you don't hang up, I'll come and sort you out personally.

Annie (*moving to Norman*) Norman . . . (*She tries to take the receiver*)

Norman (*into the phone*) What did you say? (*To Annie*) Go away.

Annie Norman—please . . .

Norman All right, Mother, I've warned you. (*Rising*) I'll come up and wrap it round your neck . . .

Norman bangs the receiver down on the table and strides out

Sarah Norman . . . (*She rises*)

Annie Norman!

Sarah Stop him . . .

Annie Norman!

Annie goes out after Norman

Sarah (*following her*) Well, don't just sit there . . .

Sarah goes out after Annie

Reg I wonder if the bloke who invented Monopoly had this trouble . . .

Tom Very difficult to concentrate. (*He rises, wanders to the phone, picks up the receiver and listens*) Good grief . . .

Reg What's happening?

Tom There's a heck of a rumpus on the extension—yelling their heads off . . . Hallo? Who's that? . . . Ruth? Oh, hallo, Ruth, it's Tom . . . Yes, Tom . . . Fine . . . How are you? . . . Oh . . . Oh . . . Oh, I see . . . Oh, I'm sorry, yes . . . Oh dear . . . Oh dear . . . (*He pulls a face at Reg*) Oh, yes . . . How dreadful . . . Yes . . .

Annie returns, breathless

Annie Tom, Reg, for goodness' sake. Leaving us to cope with Norman. He's practically attacked Mother. He's out of control.

Reg Well, I don't see that . . .

Annie Tom!

Tom What? . . . Just hang on a second, Ruth . . . (*To Annie*) What?

Annie Tom, would you stop standing there looking so useless and do something for once in your life.

Tom What?

Annie I've never met anyone so useless . . .

Tom Now look here. I wish you'd stop going on at me like this. You're damned lucky to have me around, you know.

Annie Oh, really?

Tom Yes, really. Every time anything goes wrong, you seem to take it out on me. First of all, it's your holiday, then it's Norman—well, it's just not on, it really isn't . . .

Annie Um?

Reg Won't somebody play with me, please . . .

Tom The next time you're planning holidays for two, if you want me along, perhaps you'd be good enough to be polite enough to ask me.

Annie You've got a hell of a nerve.

Tom (*pushing Annie aside as he moves to the settee table*) And, anyway, if you want to be seen with me, you'd better smarten yourself up a bit. You're a mess, you know. You look like something that's fallen off a post van.

Annie I beg your pardon?

Norman returns

Norman (*moving straight to the phone, pushing Annie out of his way*) That's settled that.

Annie Norman . . .

Norman (*into the phone*) Ruth? Hallo? . . . She's hung up. Would you believe it, she's hung up on me. (*He replaces the receiver*)

Tom I'm going home, I'm fed up. Just count yourself lucky, I don't belt you one and give you rabies.

Tom strides out to the garden.
Sarah enters with the blue bed-jacket, which now has two large holes in it

Sarah Look what you've done. Look what you've done to my bed-jacket.
Norman (*collapsing*) Nobody loves me. Nobody loves me any more.
Annie Norman . . .
Sarah Look at this. Will somebody look at this.
Reg Won't anybody play with me? Please . . .

CURTAIN

ACT II

SCENE 1

The same. Sunday, 9 p.m.

Ruth is standing by the window. Reg sits on the settee making notes about his game

Ruth I shouldn't have wasted my time coming down here. Norman makes these gestures regularly. And every time I fall for them. We've been married for five years, I really ought to know better. As a result of his hysterical phone call last night, I have not been able to do a stroke of work at home today and will probably lose my job tomorrow. When I finally turn up. I almost wish to heavens he'd gone to East Grinstead with Annie, had his week-end and got it over with. Instead of involving everyone else. Mind you, that would be much too simple for Norman. No point in making a gesture unless he has an appreciative crowd to applaud him. (*Looking at her watch*) Too late to drive back now. I think I'll go to bed in a minute.

Reg I'm amazed you two are still together.

Ruth Well. I think other people's marriages are invariably a source of amazement. They usually are to me. I mean, you and Sarah . . . You know, I have found quite often it's the people you look at and say, well, they won't last long who cling on grimly till death. Maybe they're so aware of public opinion, they're determined to prove it wrong. You and Sarah—me and Norman—and Annie and that—Tom man. Though I think Norman's successfully knocked that on the head.

Reg Tom's gone home, then?

Ruth (*looking through the magazines*) I saw him stamping off into the night. Probably the most constructive thing Norman's done for some time. Saved Annie from a fate worse than marriage. A sort of eternal engagement.

Reg I don't know. He's nice enough, Tom.

Ruth Not nice enough for her. Oh—this house! I feel like getting a paintbrush and going over it with red and orange and bright blue. It's like a brown museum. A very dirty brown museum.

Reg Well, you can't expect Annie to do anything . . .

Ruth No, I don't expect Annie to do anything. (*She sits in the easy chair with a magazine*) She's got enough to cope with, with that—evil woman upstairs.

Reg Never got on with Mother either, did you.

Ruth No. She never liked me, I never liked her. Mutual.

Reg We were saying earlier, you and Mother were rather alike.

Ruth (*laughing*) Maybe . . .

Reg I wouldn't say Sarah and I were altogether incompatible. We have differences. I won't try and hide that. We certainly have differences. But you know, six of one . . . She's pretty good with the children. On her good days. Runs the house very well. Better than you or Annie would. Or Mother.

Ruth Of course, she does have the advantage of you running round in circles for her.

Reg That's all right, I don't mind. I prefer being told what to do really. I often think if nobody told me what to do I'd never do anything at all. I remember she went away once for a fortnight. When her father was ill. Took the children with her. Left me on my own in the house. Do you know I felt myself gradually slowing down. At the end of ten days I was hardly moving at all. Extraordinary. It was as if she'd wound me up before she left and now I was running down. I hadn't even got the energy to take the milk in. Sarah reckons I've got some rare tropical disease. Burmese inertia, or something. Anyway, it's better to be calm with Sarah. She's like those toy animals you see in the back windows of cars. Any violent movement from me and she's nodding her head reproachfully for days.

Ruth leaves the magazines by the chair, rises, goes to the settee table and looks at another one

It works all right. Most days.

Annie enters and sits in the easy chair, taking off her shoes

Ruth Who's washing up?

Annie Nobody. I'm not so nobody is. I've done quite enough this weekend. I'm not doing any more.

Ruth Good for you. (*She sits on the settee with the magazine*)

Reg I'll do it in a minute.

Annie No, don't. You did it last night. Somebody else can do it.

Ruth You looking at me?

Annie Or Norman. Or Sarah.

Ruth Ha!

Reg Huh!

Annie I don't know who ever does anything in your house. You and Norman are both as bad as each other.

Ruth continues to read her magazine, holding it a few inches from her nose

Annie What are you doing?

Ruth Trying to read.

Annie You can't read like that. It's resting on your nose.

Ruth I like the smell of newsprint.

Annie Why don't you wear your glasses?

Ruth I can manage, thank you.

Annie If you don't like glasses, you could get contact lenses.

Ruth I tried them. They don't work.

Annie Of course they do.

Ruth They weren't designed for people who share a house with Norman. Life with him is full of sudden, unexpected eye movements. They kept falling out. Where the hell did you get all these dreadful magazines?

Reg They're Sarah's.

Ruth Oh. I do beg your pardon.

A pause

Reg Tom's gone home.

Annie Yes.

Reg Ah.

A pause

He'll be back tomorrow, I expect.

Annie I doubt it. Even he has a limit.

Reg Oh, he'll be back.

Ruth It's not altogether our fault if he doesn't come back.

Annie What, after the way everyone's treated him? All right, I know I haven't been particularly nice either—but that was different. I don't know why I'm so mean to him sometimes. It's just when you're fond of someone—you are enough to worry what other people think of them. You want them to be something they're not capable of being. Which is very unfair on them really. I mean, he's Tom, isn't he? That's one of the best things about him. He's always Tom. He never pretends. He never puts on an act for anybody.

Ruth No, he's always Tom. You're right there.

Annie Well, it's better than living with an emotional big-dipper like Norman.

Ruth Depends on your tastes, doesn't it?

Annie I know which I'd prefer.

Ruth Then I should stick to it then, if I were you.

Annie All right. I'm sorry. We have been through that. Norman caught me when I was very depressed. The tale end of that awful Christmas. He asked me at a time when I hardly knew what I was doing.

Ruth There's no need to explain. He's always been an expert at timing—whatever else. He proposed to me in a crowded lift. It was total blackmail. He sounded so appealing he won the sympathy of everyone round us. Had I been heartless enough to refuse him, they'd have probably dropped me down the lift shaft. I managed to stall him for three floors and then the lift man said, "Sorry, folks, nobody gets out till the little lady says yes". I remember that was the first time I really felt like throttling Norman.

Reg Very romantic. I proposed to Sarah just out there in the garden, you know.

Annie Yes, we know. Ruth and I watched you through the window.

Reg You didn't, did you?

Ruth We weren't going to tell him.

Annie Oh, what's it matter now. Sarah was all wobbly and quivering, trying to make up her mind and Ruth kept saying say no, say no.

Reg Thank you.

Annie I must see to Mother in a minute.

Ruth If it's not too tactless a question, how long is she going to remain like that?

Annie Oh, for ever. Well, till she dies.

Ruth Is that what Dr Whatsisname says?

Annie Wickham says there's no reason why she shouldn't last for years. Most of it's psychosomatic. Well, we knew that anyway. She just has no desire to get up. No reason to. So she doesn't. Sad, really. Her whole life was centred round men, wasn't it? When they lost interest in her, she lost interest in herself. I hope I never get like that.

Ruth No danger. Don't worry.

Annie Oh well, yes, I know I'm not quite the *femme fatale* figure but . . .

Ruth (*rising to take another magazine*) I mean that, thank God, you can see a bit further than she ever could. That woman never had a thought in her head in her life. Look at her, lying up there reading those dreadful books.

Annie I'm afraid if I'm here alone with her much longer, I might start to get like her. You know, when I went up to her this afternoon, I had this dress on and a bit of make-up—she was so gleeful. She thought at last her propaganda was beginning to have an effect.

Ruth Well, we'll try and come down more often. If we can. But I've got Norman and Reg has got Mrs Reg and all the little Reggies. You do see.

Annie If you could try.

Ruth Yes, we'll try. Won't we, Reg? (*She sits on the window-seat*)

Reg What? Oh, yes. Bit of a job getting away but I'll see what Sarah can arrange.

Sarah comes in

Sarah Well. (*She sits on the settee*) Nice and quiet for once.

Annie Yes . . .

Sarah What are you doing, Reg?

Reg I'm just . . .

Sarah Oh. Haven't you got anything to do?

Reg I'm doing something.

Sarah Yes—well, don't be too anti-social, will you?

A pause

I've got Norman doing the washing up.

Ruth You've what?

Annie You've really been working the charm.

Sarah No, I just had to ask him. I said would he be very kind since I wasn't feeling really up to it and—he was perfectly agreeable.

Ruth You must pass on the secret. Everything that can fall to bits in our house has done so. All the doorknobs come off in your hand. None of the cupboards open, three of the windows are stuck, the fridge needs a plug and on wet days, we have to climb out of the front-room window to go to work because the front door warps when it rains. I could probably do it myself but I'm damned if I'm going to.

Sarah If you don't mind my saying so, I think you just handle Norman wrongly. If you ask him nicely, he's very willing and helpful.

Annie That's good coming from you. You always say he's impossible.

Sarah I think we underestimate Norman.

Annie What have you been up to out there?

Sarah What do you mean?

Ruth Better change the subject.

Sarah I don't know what you mean,

Norman enters with the salad basket

Norman Excuse me.

Reg. Hey hey. The domestic man.

Norman Liberated to the kitchen.

Annie Just sling it on top of the cupboard.

Norman Sling it, right.

Annie Just gently, Norman, don't get carried away.

Norman Right-ho, Chief.

Norman salutes and goes

Ruth What a revolting sight. What have you done with the slob I married.

Annie She's house-trained him at last.

Ruth That I doubt. (*Rising*) Well, on that awful picture I'm going to bed. Which room was Norman untidying last night?

Annie The spare room. Reg's old one.

Ruth Right. Tell Norman, if he wants to join me he may. But I'd prefer it if he came on his own. (*Waving her magazine at Sarah*) May I borrow this to read?

Sarah Of course.

Ruth It's so gruesome, it should frighten me to sleep. Good night, all.

Annie Do you want a call in the morning?

Ruth If you sleep with Norman, you wake at dawn. Be warned.

Ruth goes out

Sarah Good night.

Reg 'Night.

Annie 'Night. (*She looks at one of the magazines*)

Sarah Personally, I think if she showed Norman a little more kindness and encouragement she might find him a little less difficult . . .

Annie Well, don't let one success go to your head.

Sarah Let's face it, Ruth's always had difficulty getting on with anybody. Most of the time she doesn't try.

Unseen by Sarah, Ruth returns for her handbag

I'm sure Norman's difficult to live with. I've no doubt. But any man who had to live with Ruth for any length of time . . .

Reg clears his throat

No, I mean honestly I . . . (*She tails off as she sees Ruth*)
Ruth Good night.

Ruth goes out

Sarah (*in an undertone*) She did that deliberately.
Reg (*rising*) Well, I think I'll follow on. Do you mind if I go in the bathroom first?
Sarah No.
Reg Got to drive in the morning. Get an early night.
Sarah Would you switch on the blanket, dear?
Reg Right. Do you want a bottle?
Sarah No, it's too mild for a bottle. I just want the chill off the sheets. They seemed a little damp last night.
Reg Right. (*He goes to peck Sarah on the cheek. They bump noses*) See you up there then.
Sarah All right.
Annie 'Night, Reg.

Reg goes out

Sarah I don't know when we'll get down here again. I think we're very booked up between now and Christmas.
Annie Oh well, if you can. You know . . .
Sarah It would be so much easier if we could bring the children . . .
Annie Well, do, there's room for them.
Sarah Oh, no. They'd disturb Mother.
Annie She wouldn't mind. She'd like to see them.
Sarah No. I don't think so, really. They're very noisy. We'll all come down again at Christmas, if Mother's any better. (*Pause*) I hope Tom isn't too upset.
Annie Don't know.
Sarah I expect he'll be back.
Annie Expect so.
Sarah I mean, he must realize it wasn't anything serious between you and Norman.
Annie Maybe, maybe.
Sarah I mean, as Norman says, it was just an idiotic idea of his.
Annie Did he say that?
Sarah Yes, he was saying in the kitchen, it was nothing in the least serious.

He just thought you looked a bit tired and fed up and needed a change. Act of charity, really.

Annie Oh. Is that what he said?

Sarah Nothing for Tom to get jealous about.

Annie No.

Sarah Why don't you go up to bed, too. You're looking very washed out.

Annie I have to see to Mother first.

Sarah I'll tell you what, I'll see to Mother. You get an early night for once.

Annie All right. You may have to read to her, I warn you.

Sarah I don't mind. I'll read to her.

Annie You wait till you see what she reads.

Sarah (*hustling her along*) All right then, come on, up you go.

Annie Yes, I'm going. (*She remains sitting, looking at the magazine*)

Sarah What's Mother due for, now?

Annie (*consulting her watch*) Er—nine-thirty. Two green ones and one pink if she'll swallow it. Try and persuade her to. She's got a thing about the pink ones for some reason. She says they make her giddy.

Sarah (*hurrying to the door*) Two green, one pink. (*Turning*) Coming?

Annie Yes. All right. I'm coming . . .

Sarah (*hovers for a second, then reluctantly gives up*) Well. Don't stay down too long. (*She switches out the pendant, depriving Annie of most of her reading light*) Good night.

Annie 'Night. (*She stands indeterminate. She wanders to the window and looks out unhappily*) Oh. Hell . . . (*She goes to the bookcase*) Read it— read it—read it—read it . . . (*She goes to the pile of magazines and starts to select one*)

Norman comes in with a saucepan

Norman Er—oh.

Annie On the wall. Over the draining-board, there's a hook.

Norman A hook. Right. Everyone gone to bed?

Annie Yes.

Norman It's too bad, you know, I'm slaving away out there. Ruth gone to bed?

Annie Yes. She said you're welcome to join her.

Norman Oh.

Annie Which I think is very reasonable of her, really. I'm not sure I'd be as generous.

Norman You've really gone off me, haven't you?

Annie Just a bit, Norman, yes.

Norman What can I do?

Annie I think we don't talk about it. I think we just keep out of each other's way. You'll be going home tomorrow morning then we can forget all about it.

Norman I was going to take you away, you know.

Annie I don't want to talk about it, Norman.

Norman I would have done. I was ready. I had it all planned. It was you.
You said . . .

Annie (*going to pick up her shoes*) Good night, Norman. (*She goes to the door*)

Norman Annie. Just a second, please . . .

Annie (*turning*) Good night.

Norman I didn't mean to mess it up for you and Tom, I really didn't.

Annie That's all right. You didn't.

Norman But he's gone off.

Annie I did that myself.

Norman Then why are you blaming me for it?

Annie Because as I say, Norman, I feel like I've been taking part in one
of Reg's games. Only in this case, you and Ruth are making up all the
rules as you go along.

Norman What's Ruth got to do with it? She would never have known.

Annie Until you phoned her.

Norman I only phoned her when you changed your mind. I got drunk. I
was unhappy. Oh, Annie, I wanted this week-end for you. I wanted it
to be . . .

Annie An act of charity.

Norman What?

Annie Nor do I like you discussing me in the kitchen with Sarah. Making
out you'd taken pity on me, for God's sake.

Norman Who told you that?

Annie Sarah told me. If you want a secret kept don't tell Sarah in future.

Norman I only said that to calm her down. You know what Sarah's like.
Gets all het up . . .

Annie I'm going to have an early night, Norman, I'm off.

Norman I was really looking forward to our week-end, you know.

Annie So was I.

Norman Sorry.

Annie Not all your fault.

Norman Another time, eh?

Annie Not on your life.

Norman (*sitting on the settee arm*) Oh. If I booked early enough, I could
perhaps get us into Hastings next year.

Annie Oh, Norman.

Norman I mean, not that there's anything wrong with East Grinstead
but . . .

Annie Good night.

Norman Annie. (*He falls back on the settee, looking up at her*)

Annie (*coming back into the room*) What?

Norman Can I kiss you good night?

Annie No.

Norman Can I kiss you good-bye then? Please.

Annie Norman. You are definitely evil.

Norman I love you.

Annie No.

Norman Kiss?
Annie Not until you take that back.
Norman What?
Annie That you love me. It's not true. Don't say it.
Norman All right. I don't love you. Can I have a kiss, please?
Annie Okay. Come on.

Norman hesitates

Come and get it if you want it.
Norman Don't say it like that.
Annie Well, how am I supposed to say it?
Norman Well. Nicely. Like you did at Christmas.
Annie All right. Kiss me, Norman.
Norman No.
Annie What?
Norman Come over here, first. On our rug.
Annie Now don't you start that.
Norman No, no. Just a kiss. Promise.
Annie I don't trust you.
Norman Look, I'm holding a saucepan.
Annie What's that got to do with it?
Norman I've only got one hand.
Annie I seem to remember you can do a lot with one hand.
Norman Promise.
Annie Just one kiss.
Norman Yes.
Annie (*moving to him*) Good night and good-bye, Norman.

They kiss. A little longer than Annie had planned. Norman's saucepan flails in the air

Sarah enters. She carries a pill bottle. She sees Annie and Norman. She pauses for a second and then, banging down the bottle, advances furiously and swiftly across the room

Norman sees Sarah over Annie's shoulder and tries to pull out of the kiss, with a muffled warning. He is too late. Sarah grabs Annie by the shoulder and shoves her away from Norman

Sarah You deceitful little whore. Get upstairs. Get up to bed this instant.
Annie (*amazed*) Who do you think you're talking to?
Sarah (*shoving Annie again*) Get upstairs! Go on . . .
Annie And, please, I do not like being pushed around.
Sarah I will push you around just as much as I . . .
Annie You will not, you know.
Sarah (*pushing Annie again*) Get upstairs, do you hear me? Get upstairs.
Annie I warn you, Sarah, you push me once more, I'll slap your stupid face.
Norman I say . . .

Annie And you can shut up, too, Norman

Sarah You're a really nasty piece of work, aren't you? All that innocent little girl act. You're just a tart like your Mother.

Annie Sarah, I will not have you talking about my Mother like that.

Sarah Dirty little slut.

Annie If you call me any more names . . .

Sarah Slut, slut.

Annie (*raising a rather impressive looking fist*) You asked for it.

Annie advances menacingly on Sarah. Sarah retreats

Sarah Don't you come near me. Don't you dare threaten me.

Annie Then take it back.

Ruth enters. She is now dressed only in an old dressing-gown, Norman's

Ruth stands for a moment bemused, taking in the scene, Annie and Sarah about to come to blows and Norman beginning to enjoy every minute of it

Sarah I will not take it back. You're a tart and a slut.

Annie Don't you call me that, you frustrated bitch.

Sarah Keep away. Keep away . . .

Annie I'll ring your stupid neck.

Ruth (*thundering*) Annie! Sarah! That's enough.

A silence

All right, that's enough.

Sarah (*quite hysterical*) She has no right to say that to me.

Ruth (*sharply*) I said that's enough. Good night, Sarah.

Sarah If you'd seen what she . . .

Ruth Good night, Sarah.

Sarah goes to the door, gives a last indignant glare back into the room and goes out

Good night, Annie.

Annie (*taking her shoes and going slowly to the door*) Good night.

Norman (*lamely*) 'Night.

Annie goes out

A very long silence. Ruth seems lost for words. She opens her mouth to speak to Norman, then does not. She walks up and down. She opens her mouth to speak to him again. She cannot. She walks about some more

Ruth (*finally*) Do you ever realize, Norman, the number of times in a day I could lose my temper with you and don't?

Norman continues to study his toes and the saucepan

I usually manage by some supreme effort of will to control it. Well,

this time, I'm sorry, I'm quite unable to. (*Moving to him*) You understand what I'm saying, Norman? I am simply bloody livid. (*She slaps
his face*)

Norman Ow.

Ruth How could you, Norman, how could you do it? Don't you think it
was bad enough for me at Christmas to lie there ill in bed? Knowing you
were down here playing around with not one woman, but two.

Norman (*muttering*) I wasn't playing with two.

Ruth Why do you do it? Don't you have any feeling for me?

Norman I don't know, I'm just . . .

Ruth Just what?

Norman I'm just magnetic or something.

Ruth You are not magnetic, Norman. Not at all. You are odious. You
are deceitful, odious, conceited, self-centred, selfish, inconsiderate and
shallow.

Norman I'm not shallow.

Ruth Have you anything to say at all? Anything?

Norman That's my dressing-gown, isn't it?

Ruth moves around agitatedly for a second

Ruth I don't know what to say. I just don't know what to say . . . And stop
looking like that, for heaven's sake.

Norman Like what?

Ruth Giving me that awful doggie look of yours. It may work wonders
with those two but it does nothing for me. I've seen it far too much.

*Ruth sits away from him, on the settee. Norman wanders unhappily, and
puts the saucepan on the settee table*

Well, I think this is it, don't you? I think this is where we say thank you
very much, good-bye. On top of everything else you've made me look
a complete fool . . . (*Peering round*) Where have you gone, I can't see
you?

Norman Over here.

Ruth Oh. No, I think you're just contemptible.

Norman (*edging towards her and finally touching her hand*) I'm sorry.

Ruth Don't.

Norman I am.

Ruth Let go of my hand.

Norman I am.

Ruth Will you let go of my hand.

Norman Why?

Ruth Because I don't want you touching me.

Norman Oh. (*He wanders away*) So you want me to go, do you?

Ruth I think it's the only thing left.

Norman For you.

Ruth And for you. You're obviouly not made to be married. You never
were. Stupid of me to try and make you behave like a husband in the

first place. You'd be much happier if you were perfectly free, flitting from woman to woman as the mood takes you.

Norman I don't do that.

Ruth You'd like to.

Norman I know the real reason.

Ruth Reason for what?

Norman Why you want to get rid of me. Because I interfere with your work. That's why you'd like to get rid of me.

Ruth Talk about turning the conversation. You really are the limit.

Norman Well . . .

Ruth That isn't true, either.

Norman Which comes first then? Which comes first? Work or me?

Ruth You do. Did.

Norman Work or me?

Ruth I've said, you.

Norman Work or me?

Ruth I'm not going on with this.

Norman You can't, can you? You know it's not true.

Ruth We'll talk about this in the morning. You can sleep down here.

Norman Where?

Ruth I don't know. In a chair. You're certainly not coming up with me. I refuse to be number three in a night.

Norman Nothing happened, you know. They both just started fighting. I was just saying good night to Annie and then Sarah attacked her.

Ruth Oh, yes, really? How interesting. That sounds so terribly likely.

Norman It's true. You're the only one, Ruth. You know that.

Ruth I certainly don't.

Norman Well, you should know that. You should know me by now. I mean, this whole week-end was—for you.

Ruth For me? What do you mean it was for me?

Norman It was a gesture for you.

Ruth Really.

Norman Of course it was. You know that.

Ruth (*studying him*) I don't think you're any of those things I said you were. You're just stupid.

Norman Possibly.

Ruth You just don't think. You want locking up. All right, then.

Norman What?

Ruth Come on. Come upstairs if you're coming. (*Moving to the door*) I must be half-witted but still . . . (*She waits*) Come on.

Norman (*moving to the rug and smiling*) Here a minute.

Ruth What?

Norman Just come here a second.

Ruth (*moving in slightly*) What for?

Norman Please . . .

Ruth (*moving in further*) Why?

Norman (*beckoning her in*) Bit closer—closer—that's it.

Ruth Now, I'm not in the mood for games, Norman.

Norman No. That's it. (*He draws her to him and kisses her*) I love you.
Ruth You really are the most . . .

Norman starts to pull her down on to the rug

  What are you doing?
Norman I suddenly had this wonderful idea.
Ruth What?
Norman On the rug. Come on, on the rug.
Ruth What?
Norman On the rug. Come on.
Ruth Norman, no . . .
Norman It's nice on the rug—come on, on the rug.
Ruth Norman—really.

He kisses her

Norman There. Isn't it nice on the rug?
Ruth Norman . . .
Norman Oh, Ruth . . .

They kiss and roll over

Ruth It's nice on the rug.
Norman I told you it was. It can be our rug.
Ruth Norman . . .

The lights fade as they enjoy the rug and each other

CURTAIN

SCENE 2

The same. Monday, 8 a.m.

*Ruth and Norman are now rolled up in the rug asleep. Norman's jacket is a
pillow. Reg enters without seeing them. He carries two suitcases. He places
one on the floor, puts the other on the table and starts packing away his game.
Ruth flings out her arm and hits Reg's leg. Reg jumps. He turns and sees her*

Reg Flipping heck!
Ruth Reg . . . ? (*Realizing where she is*) Oh, my God. Norman. Norman,
  wake up, you fool . . .
Norman (*instantly awake*) What—what—what—morning—what?
Ruth Norman . . .
Norman Oh—oh, God. Hallo, Reg. Ruth, we've overslept. (*He starts to
  try to get up*)
Ruth (*yelling*) Don't unroll the rug yet. Wait a minute.
Norman Sorry. Oh yes . . .

Ruth and Norman wriggle about under the rug adjusting their dress

Ruth (*as they do so*) You don't really have to stand there gaping, do you, Reg?

Reg Oh, no. Sorry, no. 'Morning. (*He continues packing up the game*)

Ruth (*satisfied that her dressing-gown is again covering her*) All right.

Norman Right.

They unroll from the rug

Ruth Honestly. (*She gets up*) You fool, Norman. Why didn't you wake up? Please, Reg, don't say anything to anyone, will you? I beg you. I'll never live it down.

Reg No—no . . .

Ruth Honestly, Norman, you fool. Why didn't you wake up?

Ruth goes out

Norman smiles amiably at Reg

Reg I take it you two have patched up your little differences?

Norman My wife and I have come to an agreement.

Reg Good.

Norman (*getting up*) Lovely morning—oooh! She's been lying on my arm. Oooh, oooh, oooh. (*He finds his apron backwards and twists it round*) Wouldn't tell anybody about this. (*He straightens the rug*)

Reg No.

Norman Otherwise they'll all want to do it.

Reg Don't think I fancy it. Prefer my bed. Despite the wife. (*He laughs*)

Norman You're off then?

Reg She seems to be hurrying me along for some reason, yes. What was the matter with her last night, do you know?

Norman Who?

Reg Sarah. She came to bed shaking. I've never seen her so bad. I mean, literally shaking. The whole bed was vibrating for hours. Like sleeping on top of a spin dryer.

Norman It must have been the over-excitement.

Reg What over-excitement?

Norman No idea.

Reg Not much of that this week-end was there? Well, the old arguments but that's usual. I must say, on the whole, I've enjoyed the rest.

Norman Yes. Good to get out to the countryside occasionally.

Reg You're right there.

Sarah comes in with a bag

Sarah Reg, have you brought those . . . ? Ah, yes—oh. (*She sees Norman*)

Norman 'Morning.

Sarah (*coolly*) Good morning. (*To Reg*) What are you doing?

Reg Just packing. Just packing.

Sarah (*collecting up the magazines*) Oh, we're not lugging that all the way home with us again, are we?
Reg I'm not leaving it here. This took me months to make.

Norman wanders to the door

Sarah We're never going to have time for it, Reg.
Reg It's all right, I think I've adapted it now so I can play on my own.
Sarah (*piling the magazines on the settee table*) And you promised to take these magazines up to Mother.
Reg I will. I'm going to. I'll have my breakfast first.
Sarah (*picking up the saucepan*) And we can't waste too much time over that, either. (*Coldly to Norman, who is blocking the way out*) Excuse me, please.

Sarah goes out

Reg What's the hurry? We're in a hurry. I don't think she's forgiven you yet, by the look of it.
Norman No.
Reg No. Very cool. Got a long memory has Sarah. It'll be a few months before you're back in favour.
Norman Ah well. I'll try and win her round.
Reg No chance. You'll be told when you're forgiven and not before. She doesn't talk to me for days on end sometimes. Amazing how she remembers to keep it up. I mean, if I have a row in the morning, when I come home in the evening I've forgotten all about it. Until I open the front door. Then it hits you straightaway. Atmosphere like a rolling-pin. Know what I mean? She's got great emotional stamina, my wife.
Norman So have I.
Reg You'll need it. Good luck.

Norman goes out

Reg, alone, whistles a tune, wanders to the centre of the room, looks at the rug and laughs. He wanders to the window and stares out

Reg Oh, hallo. What are you doing out there?

Tom comes in from the garden rather tentatively

Tom Ah . . .
Reg What were you doing hiding out there? Thought you were a cat burglar. (*He laughs*)
Tom No. Er—thought I'd just look in, you know. I was on my way to—somewhere—and I thought I'd look in.
Reg Come in. (*He goes to the magazine pile and tidies it*)
Tom Thank you.

Tom picks up a magazine, Reg puts it back, several times

Reg Nice day again.

Tom Um?

Reg Lovely.

Tom I'm afraid I flew off the handle last night.

Reg Oh, don't worry.

Tom I shouldn't think I'll be very welcome here today.

Reg Why ever not? Don't worry . . .

Tom I didn't sleep at all. Turning it over in my mind, you know. I mean, let's face it. What claim have I got to Annie? None at all. Why should I kick up a fuss—if somebody else . . .

Reg It's natural. Human nature.

Tom I shouldn't have blown my top.

Reg I don't honestly think a lot of people noticed.

Tom Really?

Reg No.

Tom I was very boorish.

Reg Well . . .

Annie comes in dressed as in Act I, Scene 1

Annie Oh. Hallo.

Tom Hallo.

Annie There's some tea and stuff in there, if you want it, Reg.

Reg Oh, right-ho. Wonderful.

Annie Not a lot but . . .

Reg Right. (*Pause*) I think I'll take these up to Mother. Before I forget. Otherwise Sarah'll be on to me again. Excuse me.

Reg picks up the pile of magazines and goes out

Tom Yes. I must be getting along, I think. I was just . . .

Annie Tom.

Tom Yes.

Annie Stay a minute.

Tom All right. (*He looks at his watch*) Yes, fine. (*He looks at his watch again*) Fine. I came to apologize really.

Annie What for?

Tom Well, for—yesterday—losing my temper and—general things.

Annie No need to apologize.

Tom No, I know there isn't. Everyone keeps telling me that. But I think an apology's due. I came to give it. To you.

Annie Thank you.

Tom Well. (*He looks at his watch*) Well . . .

Annie Do you want a cup of tea before you go?

Tom Oh. If there's one going. Won't say no. Didn't feel like breakfast when I got up. Felt a bit sick actually, but—er . . .

Annie Come on then.

Tom You think they'll—er—welcome me in there?

Annie Why ever not? Come on. (*She starts to lead Tom out*)

Ruth enters as Tom and Annie reach the door. She is now dressed, and is carrying Norman's case, jacket, overcoat and woolly cap. The medals have been removed from the jacket

Tom Oh, Ruth, I—er . . .
Ruth Oh hallo, Tom, good morning. You're bright and early. (*She puts the case by the easy chair*)
Tom Ruth, I . . .
Ruth Mmm? (*She puts the clothes over the back of the easy chair*)
Tom I—er—nothing.
Ruth What's wrong?
Annie Nothing's wrong. Come on.
Tom Right.

Norman enters as Tom and Annie go out

Norman Hallo. Good morning, Mr Vet. (*He slaps Tom on the back*)

Tom and Annie go out

You're dressed.
Ruth (*sitting on the settee*) I wasn't going home in your dressing-gown. I've come up in a rash. I think it was from that rug.
Norman Really? That's unusual.
Ruth What do you mean unusual? Do you make a habit of rolling people on the rug?
Norman No.
Ruth No?
Norman No. You look fabulous this morning.
Ruth I look simply dreadful. I couldn't see my face. I haven't had a bath. I feel terrible.
Norman I love that dress. It's great.
Ruth It's the same one I had on yesterday.
Norman Is it?
Ruth I only brought one with me. I didn't plan to spend the night in the hearth. I suppose you want me to drive you home now?
Norman Yes, please.
Ruth I have to go to work.
Norman You'll have to go home first, you can't go to work like that. You look a dreadful mess.
Ruth Yes. You're supposed to be at work, too.
Norman I was taken ill, haven't you heard?
Ruth I'm amazed they keep you on.
Norman I'm a very good librarian, that's why. I know where all the dirty bits are in all the books.

Ruth We'd better say good-bye.

Norman No breakfast.

Ruth You can get something at home. If there is anything—which I doubt.

Norman What would you say—if I asked you a favour?

Ruth What sort of favour?

Norman Would you take the day off and stay at home?

Ruth No.

Norman Not even with me?

Ruth Especially not with you.

Norman Please.

Ruth Norman, I am doing a full-time job. I just can't . . .

Norman I could ring up for you. I could say you were ill.

Ruth No.

Norman Oh, why can't you be ill for once? Go on, be ill. I know. I'll pretend I'm the doctor. I'll say, I am phoning up on behalf of Mrs Norman Dewers. I have just examined this woman on the rug. She has an ugly rash and in my opinion, she's in great need of some attention. Attention from who, you may ask. (*He leaps to Ruth and sits on the settee*)

Ruth Norman . . .

Norman Kiss.

Ruth Norman. (*She kisses him*)

Norman Are you happy?

Ruth What?

Norman Do I make you happy at all?

Ruth Well . . .

Norman Say you're happy.

Ruth Why? Is it important?

Norman Yes. I want you to be happy. I want everyone to be happy. I want to make everyone happy. It's my mission in life . . .

Ruth Yes, all right, Norman. Well, let's not worry about other people too much, just concentrate on making me happy, will you? The other people will have to try to be happy without you, won't they?

Norman But you are happy?

Ruth Yes. I'm fairly happy.

Norman And you might possibly—feel ill—if you drove very fast all the way home and—somebody made you a cup of tea and—made the bed and—ran you a bath and—put in the bath salts and . . .

Ruth Yes. I might.

Norman How are you feeling?

Ruth Dreadful.

Norman (*with a great cry of joy*) Ha-ha! (*He grabs her*)

Reg enters with a bunch of flowers in tissue. He puts them on the settee table

Reg Oh, blimey, they're at it again.

Sarah and Annie come in

Ruth breaks from Norman

Sarah Well, I think we're ready to go.
Reg One piece of toast. One piece of toast. How can I drive on one piece of toast.

Norman puts on his jacket

Annie Have you got everything?
Sarah I think so. Did you take our sponge bag out of the bathroom, Reg?
Reg Yes, yes, yes.
Ruth Well, I'm going to see if I can start the car.
Norman Right. (*He starts to put on his mac and hat*)
Ruth Oh, Norman, you don't have to put all that on.
Norman I prefer to travel incognito.
Ruth You've still got that suit on. It isn't even yours.
Norman Oh, yes. Can I borrow this, please?
Annie Well, Father doesn't need it any more. You might as well.
Ruth It doesn't even fit him.
Norman I could do with a new executive suit.
Ruth Come on. (*To Sarah, Reg and Annie in turn*) Good-bye. Good-bye. Good-bye.
Annie 'Bye, Ruth.
Reg 'Bye, 'bye.
Sarah Good-bye.
Ruth (*going*) I'm in the car. I'm leaving in ten seconds.

Ruth exits to the garden

Norman All right. All right. (*To Annie*) Good-bye, Annie. Thank you and . . .
Annie (*fairly cool*) Good-bye, Norman.
Norman Reg.
Reg So long.
Norman Sarah. (*He shakes Sarah's hand*)
Sarah (*warmly*) Good-bye, Norman. Have a good journey. See you at Christmas, I hope.
Norman Like the mistletoe, I shall be here.
Ruth (*off*) Norman!
Norman Bag. Where's my bag?
Reg (*pointing*) That it?

Norman goes for his case

Ruth (*off*) Norman!
Sarah (*going to the door and calling*) He's just coming, Ruth, he's just coming.

Reg She's forgiven you very quickly, hasn't she?

Norman You think so?

Reg What did you say to her?

Norman Nothing. I just cheered her up a bit. 'Bye 'bye. Good-bye, Annie Good-bye, Sarah.

Ruth (*off*) Norman, I have left.

Norman All right, all right, I'm coming.

Norman goes, his hand brushing Sarah's as he passes her

Reg Well. Nice to see him, but I'm glad it's only twice a year.

Sarah Yes, I think it's time we were... Good-bye, Annie. (*She pecks Annie's cheek*) Take care, won't you?

Annie And you. Have a good journey.

Reg Thank you.

Annie You won't mind if I don't come and see you off, will you? I must get back to Tom. He's sitting there waiting. He's decided he'd like breakfast after all.

Sarah Oh, yes, you go back to Tom.

Reg Annie, I told him not to worry about this week-end. I did right, did I? To tell him that?

Annie Yes.

Reg Hope everything works out.

Annie Expect so.

Sarah (*at the window*) Norman's having to push that car of theirs.

Reg (*to Annie*) Want a tip? Take Tom out there. Sit him under the tree. Good place to make a proposal out there.

Annie It worked for you.

Reg Yes.

Annie I'll try it. One of these days. 'Bye, 'bye.

Sarah Good-bye, Annie dear.

Reg 'Bye, love.

Annie goes out to the house

Sarah Oh, I am fond of this garden. Even though it's overgrown. Oh, just look at Norman. What does he think he's doing. (*She laughs*)

Reg Could do with a lot of work. I thought they were still paying someone to look after it. That old man. He's worse than useless. No-one keeps an eye on him. So he doesn't do a stroke.

Sarah As long as the sun's shining, I'm happy.

Reg Are you? (*He picks up the cases*)

Sarah stands smiling serenely

You're very cheerful.

Sarah Why shouldn't I be?

Reg No. No reason. Carry on.

Sarah Can you manage those?

Reg Just about.

Pause

Sarah I wonder what Bournemouth would be like at this time of year?
Reg Bournemouth?
Sarah Yes.
Reg What made you suddenly think of Bournemouth?
Sarah It just occurred to me.
Reg You don't want to go to Bournemouth, do you?
Sarah Not now . . .
Reg I thought we were going home.
Sarah Not now. Sometime. I think I'd rather fancy it. Next year—perhaps.
Reg All right. I'll take you. If it'll make you happy.
Sarah No, you don't need to bother. I could go on my own easily.
Reg On your own?
Sarah Leave you in peace for a bit. Just for the week-end. Be rather nice
to get away. For a week-end . . .
Reg Don't know why you want to go to Bournemouth. Why Bourne-
mouth? Why not make it Brighton? Or Worthing? (*Sarah goes out to the
garden, taking the bunch of flowers*) Or Reigate, for that matter? Or East
Grinst . . . (*He pauses. An awful thought*) Oh, my God. Sarah! Wait for
me, love. Sarah . . .

Reg hurries out with his cases

CURTAIN

FURNITURE AND PROPERTY LIST

ACT I

SCENE 1

On stage: Pouffe
Settee with antimacassar and 2 cushions
Easy chair matching settee
Brown fur hearth rug
Coffee-table

Low round table. *On it:* telephone, notepad, pencil
Settee table. *On it:* large suitcase containing blue bed-jacket in tissue
    paper, game board and pieces, one loose piece, dressing. *Under*
    table: waste-paper basket
Dining chair
Low chair
Plant stand with plant
Stand with table lamp. *In front of it:* suitcase
Round table. *Under it:* wind-up gramophone with record in place
Bookcase with books. *On top:* lamp
In garden: wheelbarrow
On window-seat: 3 cushions

Off stage: Small battered suitcase (**Norman**)
          Bundle of magazines tied with string (**Reg**)
          3 bottles of home-made wine, 3 glasses, corkscrew (**Annie**)
          Dustpan and brush (**Annie**)

Scene 2

Off stage: Tray with 4 cups, saucers and teaspoons, coffee-pot, milk jug, sugar
          basin (**Sarah**)
          Bed-jacket with two large holes in it (**Sarah**)

ACT II

Scene 1

Strike: Coffee things
          Bottles and glasses
          Dining chair
          Low chair
          Norman's suitcase

Set: Ruth's handbag behind settee

Off stage: Salad basket (**Norman**)
          Apron (**Norman**)
          Saucepan (**Norman**)
          Pill bottle (**Sarah**)

Personal: **Reg:** notebook and pencil

Scene 2

Off stage: 2 suitcases (**Reg**)
          Norman's suitcase, mac, hat and suit jacket (**Ruth**)
          Bunch of roses in tissue paper (**Sarah**)

Personal: Wrist watch for **Sarah, Annie, Ruth, Reg, Tom**
          Sarah: handbag with handkerchief and compact
          Ruth: handbag with handkerchief and compact

LIGHTING PLOT

Property fittings required: Pendant, 2 table lamps, garden light
Interior. A living-room. The same scene throughout

ACT I, SCENE 1. Evening

To open: Effect of early summer evening light

No cues

ACT I, SCENE 2. Evening

To open: Effect of summer evening—2 hours later than above but still daylight

Cue 1   **Tom** exits to garden   (Page 17)
            Snap on garden light

ACT II, SCENE 1. Late evening

To open: All practicals on

Cue 2   **Sarah** switches off pendant   (Page 34)
            Snap off pendant and covering spots, including those over easy
               chair

Cue 3   **Ruth:** "Norman . . ."   (Page 40)
            Fade to Black-Out

ACT II, SCENE 2 Morning

To open: Effect of bright morning sunshine

No cues

EFFECTS PLOT

ACT I

SCENE 1

Cue 1   **Norman** puts on record   (Page 14)
*Music: Richard Tauber singing "Girls were made to Love
and Kiss"—continue till Curtain*

SCENE 2

No cues

ACT II

SCENE 1

Cue 2   **Ruth:** "Norman . . ."   (Page 40)
Music: Tauber record as above, as Lights fade

SCENE 2

No cues

THE NORMAN CONQUESTS

ROUND AND ROUND THE GARDEN

A Play

ALAN AYCKBOURN

SAMUEL   FRENCH

LONDON

NEW YORK   TORONTO   SYDNEY   HOLLYWOOD

Please see page iv for further copyright information

ROUND AND ROUND THE GARDEN

First presented by the Library Theatre Co., Scarborough in June 1973 and subsequently by the Greenwich Theatre Company in May 1974, and in London by Michael Codron at the Globe Theatre in August 1974, with the following cast of characters:

Norman	Tom Courtenay
Tom	Michael Gambon
Sarah	Penelope Keith
Annie	Felicity Kendal
Reg	Mark Kingston
Ruth	Bridget Turner

The play directed by Eric Thompson
Setting by Alan Pickford

The action passes in the garden of a Victorian vicarage-type house during a week-end in July

ACT I
    Scene 1   Saturday, 5.30 p.m.
    Scene 2   Saturday, 9 p.m.

ACT II
    Scene 1   Sunday, 11 a.m.
    Scene 2   Monday, 9 a.m.

Period – the present

ACT ONE

SCENE 1

The garden. Saturday, 5.30 p.m.

The garden is overlooked by a Victorian, country-vicarage-type house with terrace and french windows leading directly into the sitting-room. Once obviously well laid out, it is now wildly overgrown. There is an entrance to the tennis-court and the road, and another—above an old statue and through some brambles—which leads round to the same direction: these also go to the front of the house

Tom, a thoughtful, pensive man, enters above the statue. He is casually dressed in week-end country clothes. He stands gazing rather aimlessly about him, then wanders down to the barrel, on which is a cup and saucer. He picks up the cup, and is surprised to find the saucer stuck to it. After considering this for a moment, he replaces cup and saucer

Annie enters from the tennis-court. Red-faced and shiny, she wears a very old sweater, button-up and too large, jeans and gumboots. She also has on a pair of gardening gloves and carries six roses and a pair of scissors. She stops on seeing Tom

Annie (*casually*) Oh, Tom. Hallo.
Tom Hallo, Annie.
Annie Didn't know you were here this afternoon.
Tom Yes. I thought I'd just look up your cat if I could. See that paw of his.
Annie Oh, yes, fine.
Tom I put a dressing on it but it's probably come off by now.
Annie Probably.

A pause

Tom Lovely day.
Annie Yes.
Tom You'll be going off soon, I take it.
Annie Yes.
Tom Oh. Have a good time.
Annie Thanks.
Tom Don't get lost.
Annie I can't get far in a day. Any sign of Reg and Sarah?
Tom Haven't seen them.
Annie Hope they're not going to be late. I'll have to hang on till they come just to make sure they know where everything is for Mother.

Tom Yes.

Annie She's been lying up there moaning all day because I'm going away. You'd think I was off for a year, instead of a couple of nights.

Tom I'll look in if you like. Make sure they're coping.

Annie They'll manage.

Tom Nice of them to offer, wasn't it?

Annie Sarah and Reg?

Tom Yes.

Annie (*putting five roses on the terrace and clipping the sixth*) Why shouldn't they? She's his mother, too, after all. It's high time they did offer. They get off very lightly. So does Ruth for that matter. They're all perfectly happy to leave me to cope for nine-tenths of the year. The least they can do is to spare me a couple of days. Not that I'll ever get Ruth to do anything. Far too busy with her high finance. But Reg and Sarah are perfectly capable . . .

Tom Quite.

Annie What will you be doing?

Tom When?

Annie This week-end.

Tom Oh, you know. Mooching about.

Annie On your own?

Tom Probably.

Annie That's what I'll be doing.

Tom Ah. Well, I'll think of you, wherever you are, mooching about while I'm—mooching about here.

Annie Thanks. (*Pause*) Silly, really.

Tom What?

Annie Well—both of us in different parts of the country, stuck on our own . . .

Tom Yes. Funny thing, life.

Annie Yes. (*Pause*) What's the time?

Tom Er—just gone five-thirty.

Annie Oh.

Tom When are you leaving?

Annie I'm catching the bus in the village. That's providing Reg and Sarah arrive in time.

Tom I can run you down in the car.

Annie No . . .

Tom If you look like being . . .

Annie No, I'd rather walk.

Tom Won't you have a case?

Annie No. It's all right. I don't mind carrying suitcases. I quite enjoy it. The walk . . .

Tom Oh. Any idea where that cat is?

Annie Probably outside here somewhere. I must get on. Prepare for my lone trip.

Tom See you before you go then.

Annie Yes.

Tom Better search out my patient. (*Calling*) Pussy, puss, puss . . .

Tom goes off by the tennis-court

Annie stands for a moment looking after Tom

Annie (*at length, exasperated*) Oh . . .

Annie goes off to the house, taking the cup and saucer

A pause

Norman enters stealthily by the statue. Despite the bright sunshine of the late July afternoon, he has on a rather grimy mac and a woolly hat. He is bearded, a rather aimless sort of beard. He carries a battered cardboard suitcase. Not surprisingly, he is perspiring furiously. As the house comes into his view, he stops, smiles to himself, puts down his case and, at peace with the world, breathes in the country air

Tom (*off, distant*) Kitty—kitty—kitty—cat—cat—cat—kitty—kitty—kitty . . .

Norman, on hearing this, dives swiftly for cover, forgetting his case which he leaves standing in the middle of the path. Tom's voice fades into the distance. Norman remains hidden

Annie enters and picks up the remaining roses. She stops as she sees Norman's case. She approaches, curious, and stares at it. She looks about her

Annie Hallo? Anyone about?
Norman (*hidden, muffled*) Annie . . .

Annie stares about her

Annie . . .
Annie Norman?
Norman (*showing himself*) Annie!
Annie Oh—you've come . . .
Norman Yes.
Annie But what are you . . . ?
Norman I couldn't wait. I had to see you.
Annie But we agreed . . . Oh, Norman, honestly. You are the limit . . .
Norman (*passionately*) Oh, my darling . . . (*He moves romantically to her but stops suddenly. With a cry*) Oh—God!
Annie (*alarmed*) What's the matter?
Norman These bloody brambles. Why doesn't somebody clear these bloody brambles?
Annie Hang on—stop flailing about . . . (*She takes his hand to pull him clear*)

Norman (*yelling*) Don't pull! Don't pull! It's impaled in my leg.
Annie (*bending to free him*) All right. Wait—wait . . .
Norman Aaaah!
Annie Ssh.
Norman You must have hands like asbestos. (*As Annie frees him*) Aaah!
Aaah! Aaah! (*Hopping away and sitting on the barrel*) God!
Annie Mother's resting, you know. You'll wake her up.
Norman (*rolling up his trouser leg*) Look at this. I'm scratched right down
my leg.
Annie If Mother's woken up before she's ready to wake up, she doesn't
know where she is. It takes me an hour to explain.
Norman Look, blood—bleeding . . .
Annie Let's see. (*She bends to look*)
Norman Careful! Deformed for life.
Annie Hold these. (*She hands Norman the roses*)
Norman (*taking them and dropping them immediately with another yell*)
Aaah!
Annie Ssh.
Norman It's a death trap, this garden.
Annie Look, will you please be quiet.
Norman Only been here two minutes, lost three pints of blood. (*He sucks
his hand*)
Annie Oh, Norman, do shut up. You're so weedy.
Norman (*indignantly*) Weedy? (*He rises*)
Annie A real weed. (*She starts to pick up the flowers*)
Norman (*romantic again*) Oh, Annie . . . (*He reaches out and touches her
leg*)
Annie (*pulling away, irritated*) Don't. Just a minute.

Norman stares at her a second, then sits again

Norman I'm exhausted.
Annie I should think so. In that coat.
Norman It was raining in Fulham.
Annie Was it?
Norman Metaphorically it was.
Annie Oh.
Norman (*expansively*) Ah, the sun, the sun, the sun . . .
Annie Norman . . .
Norman Mmm?
Annie What are you doing here?

Norman laughs secretively

No, seriously, Norman. What's the point of our making all these
arrangements, of trying to make absolutely sure no-one was going to
get upset—no-one was going to get hurt and then you turn up here.
Norman I wanted to see you. I was frightened you'd changed your mind.
Annie But I'm supposed to meet you. We're supposed to meet. In the
village, at the back of the post office, seven o'clock.

Norman I got here early.

Annie Well, you'll have to go away for an hour. I haven't even packed.

Norman Where am I supposed to go?

Annie I don't know. Go and walk round the Abbey.

Norman That's five miles away. I'm not walking five miles, just to wander round some ruin with a suitcase.

Annie I don't want you here when Reg and Sarah arrive. And I've got to see them in. I've got to show them where everything is for Mother. All her bottles and pills and God knows what. And which is their towel. I mean, there's masses. I can't just rush off. Anyway, Tom's here . . .

Norman (*scornfully*) Tom.

Annie He's only round the front of the house, looking for the cat.

Norman Tom. Ha!

Annie And don't say it like that. I don't say Ruth, ha!

Norman I don't mind if you do. I say it.

Annie Not to her face, you don't.

Norman How do you know?

Annie I bet you don't. I've seen you with her.

Norman How do you know what I say to her face behind your back?

Annie I know you. More important I know my sister.

Norman She'll have got my note by now.

Annie Note?

Norman Telling all.

Annie All what?

Norman It's all over between us. That ever since we stayed here last Christmas, something wonderful happened. You and I were all that mattered. That everything else . . .

Annie You didn't? You didn't say that?

Norman That the love between us . . .

Annie If you said that, I warn you, I'll ring her up this minute . . . (*She moves away*)

Norman (*alarmed*) Where are you going?

Annie To ring her up.

Norman All right, all right. I didn't. I didn't leave her a note. Promise.

Annie Promise?

Norman Promise.

Annie So long as you haven't. I mean—well, after all she is my sister. I'm fond of her. Quite. We've already agreed it's stupid to—upset everything just for us. We're being terribly adult, aren't we? You said we were—in your letter . . . Far better we two just go away quietly to a little hotel somewhere, get it all off our chests—out of our system—God, I'm making it sound like a laxative—you know what I mean—work it all off, that's what I mean. Then you go back to Ruth and live happily ever after—or as happily as you can seeing it's Ruth and I come back to Mother and—and—look after her . . .

Norman And then? When your mother finally pegs out?

Annie Oh well. I'll face that when it comes.

Norman Yes, you'll have to.

Annie There's Tom. He's hovering in the background.
Norman The creeping vet.
Annie He's done a lot to help here, you know. He did all the kitchen
ceiling for me. Two coats. He's a jolly good vet, too. He has a marvel-
lous way with animals. Actually, he's better with them than he is with
people really.
Norman You'll have to start going around on all fours then, won't you.
Annie Oh, shut up. I don't know why you're so nasty about him, he likes
you very much.
Norman He takes you for granted. Here you are—a beautiful girl. Vibrant.
He could marry you tomorrow. He could make you happy. And what
does he do? He spends more time with that cat than he does with you.
Annie Well, he's a vet, isn't he?
Norman Vet. V.E.T. Very Egocentric Twit. He doesn't deserve you.
Annie And you do?
Norman No. But I'm strangely engaging.
Annie No, you're not, you're foul. I don't think I want to come with you
after all. I've changed my mind. I'll give Mother a blanket bath, it'll be
much more fun.
Norman I love you.
Annie Oh, Norman . . . When you look like that, I almost believe you.
You look like a—what are those things?
Norman Greek gods. (*He does a "Greek god" attitude*)
Annie Old English sheepdogs.
Norman Oh, great.
Annie They're super dogs. All woolly and double-ended.
Norman I'm not woolly and double-ended.
Annie You are a bit. You're like a badly built haystack.
Norman I'm going.
Annie Yes, you'd better before Tom . . .
Norman (*taking her hand, suddenly very serious and intense*) Good-bye, my
darling.
Annie (*suppressing her laughter*) Oh, Norman, do stop it.
Norman What?
Annie Oh, I'm sorry, I . . . (*She starts laughing*)
Norman (*hurt*) What?
Annie It's just you're so—terribly quaint.
Norman (*huffily*) If it's quaint to be romantic . . . I mean, if you prefer
me to knock you down . . .
Annie Try it.
Norman If that's what you want. Where's the romance? Where's the
romance gone? Destroyed by the cynics and liberationists. Woe betide
the man who dares to pay a woman a compliment today—he bends to
kiss her hand and wham—the old karate chop on the back of the neck
and she's away with his wallet. Forget the flowers, the chocolates, the
soft word—rather woo her with a self-defence manual in one hand and a
family planning leaflet in the other.
Annie Oh, Norman, you are stupid.

Norman Yes. I really do love you, Annie.

Annie Do you?

Norman Yes.

Annie That's a pity.

Norman Why?

Annie For everyone. Golly, look at this garden. It's like a jungle. Old Mr Purdy's got his leg again. He's been off a fortnight.

Norman (*uninterested*) Oh.

Annie Mrs Purdy says it's a war wound but I think it's gout. He's a terrific drinker. All day. The potting shed's full of his empties. He says they're for weed killer but he's got enough there to defoliate the whole of Sussex. If you look out of the window at tea time, you can see him draped over his spade. Like an old bag of fertilizer . . .

Norman Seven o'clock, then, back of the post office. (*He goes to move*)

Annie Seven o'clock. I say, it's awfully exciting in a way, isn't it? I mean, do you know I haven't been away from this place for nearly two years, what with Mother and one thing and another. I'm longing to see the sea again. I've forgotten what it looks like.

Norman Ah.

Annie Where did you say we were going? Hastings. Why did you choose Hastings?

Norman Well—it looks sort of close on the map.

Annie I'm not complaining. I mean, I'm sure Hastings is super.

Norman Yes. As a matter of fact, I wasn't able to get a vacancy after all —not in Hastings.

Annie Oh.

Norman It's summer, you see.

Annie Yes, I've noticed.

Norman Ah, well, I'd forgotten.

Annie So we're not going to Hastings?

Norman I'm afraid not.

Annie Where are we going?

Norman Well, I managed after a bit of trouble to get us fixed up in East Grinstead. They had a cancellation.

Annie (*digesting this*) Oh, well. Super. East Grinstead, then. I haven't been there, either.

Norman It was the best I could do. It's on the way to Hastings.

Annie Lovely.

Norman (*leering*) Not that we'll see much of it—eh?

Annie (*blankly*) How do you mean?

Norman Well . . .

Annie Oh. (*Doubtfully*) Oh, yes. (*She thinks*) I expect we'll want some fresh air at some stage though, won't we? I mean, we won't—all the time. I mean, if it's a hotel they'll want to make the beds and change the soap—so I expect we'll get time for a bit of a snoop around, just a bit.

Norman (*unconvinced*) Oh, yes . . .

Annie It'd be a shame to go all the way to East Grinstead and then not

see anything of it at all. I mean, what the hell, let's do what we said
and have a really *dirty* week-end. I mean, absolutely *filthy* but, you know,
if it's all . . . Makes Jill a dull girl. (*She laughs*) God, I'm putting this
awfully badly.

Norman You've just pulled a button off.

Annie Mmm?

Norman Your woolly thing. You've just pulled the button off.

Annie (*finding it in her hand, absently*) Oh, yes. (*She puts the button in her
pocket*)

They are both embarrassed now

Norman I stopped off in the village. Bought some new pyjamas.

Annie Oh. Super. In my honour?

Norman Yes.

Annie Better than wearing the same ones you do with Ruth.

Norman Yes.

Annie I mean, just because you're unfaithful there's no need for your
pyjamas to be as well.

Norman No.

Annie I'm afraid you'll have to put up with my sensible flannelette.
They're quite pretty but they're going round the knees and elbows.

Norman Ah.

A pause

Annie Well.

Norman Yes.

A pause

Would you like to have a look at my pyjamas now?

Annie Well, I . . .

Norman A sort of sneak preview.

Annie I think I'd rather wait until . . . (*She pauses—listens*) Was that the
bell?

Norman Bell?

Annie Ssh. Mother's bell. She's awake. Now, you must go. See you at
seven. (*As she hurries into the house*) I'll have a bath before I leave.

Annie goes into the house

*Norman stares after her. He stands looking uncertain. He opens his case
and removes a pair of cellophane-wrapped pyjamas. He stares at them
critically. He places them on the statue and steps back to see what effect
they have from a distance*

Tom (*off*) Kitty—kitty—kitty . . .

Norman hides behind the statue

Tom enters from the tennis-court

Cat—cat—cat—kitty—kitty—kitty. (*He spies the cat up a tall tree*) Ah, there you are.

Norman appears, staring in disbelief. Tom turns from looking up at the tree, sees the case, stares at it, turns, and sees Norman

Oh, hallo, Norman. Didn't know you were here.

Norman Tom. (*He shakes Tom's hand*)

Tom You and Ruth down to lend a hand, are you?

Norman How do you mean?

Tom With Annie going away. Are you down to help out?

Norman More or less.

Tom Where's Ruth?

Norman She's not here.

Tom Oh. I thought you said she was.

Norman No, I never said she was. You're the one who said she was.

Tom (*deciding he has lost the thread of this conversation*) Look at that daft animal.

Norman Mmm?

Tom See it? The cat—up there.

Norman Oh, yes.

Tom (*calling*) Avoiding me—aren't you? (*To Norman*) Septic paw.

Norman Uggh.

Tom Last time I looked at it, we two had a mild disagreement. (*To the cat*) Didn't we? Yes. (*To Norman*) Not the most sociable animal.

Norman Vicious brute. Kills on sight for pleasure.

Tom Well, I can't really treat a patient who's thirty foot up a tree. Think I'll call it a day. No way of luring him down.

Norman You could sling a brick at it.

Tom Hardly.

Norman Breach of professional etiquette?

Tom Something of the sort. (*Seeing Norman's pyjamas*) Good Lord, what on earth are those?

Norman Ssh. They look like wild pyjamas. Don't disturb them, they're nesting.

Tom Yours, are they?

Norman Yes. I better put them away before they savage someone. (*Snatching them, pretending they are attacking him, then cramming them back in the suitcase*) Go on, get in you brutes. In, in—get in. (*He slams the lid triumphantly*) The tops are all right, it's the bottoms you've got to watch.

Tom (*impassive through this*) Seen Annie yet?

Norman No. Yes. Why?

Tom Well. What's your opinion?

Norman What of?

Tom Man to man? Between you and me?

Norman What?

Tom I mean, it's very odd, isn't it?

Norman What is?

Tom Her holiday. I mean, there's nothing wrong in having a holiday, but why the mystery?

Norman Mystery?

Tom Practically sneaking off. Won't say where she's going. What she's going to do.

Norman Perhaps she doesn't want people to know.

Tom Not like Annie, that. She's usually very open. Frank sort of person. No secrets. Know what I mean?

Norman Really.

Tom I mean, I've known her a long time . . .

Norman That doesn't give you ownership of her.

Tom No. Gives me interest. Concern.

Norman I should stick to coaxing cats out of trees.

Tom (*thoughtfully*) Hastings.

Norman Eh?

Tom I've got a feeling she's set her sights on Hastings.

Norman Oh?

Tom She keeps bringing it up. In passing. You know—"Do you think it'll be warm in Hastings at this time of year?"—that sort of thing. Sometimes she tries to confuse the scent. Makes it Deal or Brighton. But Hastings is the commonest. I'm betting even money on Hastings. (*Calling*) Pussy—pussy—puss. This question is—and I'd like your advice on this, Norman . . . (*He pauses, gazing up into the tree*) The point is, Norman, should I or should I not offer to go to Hastings, too? I've been turning it over in my mind, should I or shouldn't I?

Norman No.

Tom Why is she going, I ask myself. Is she going as a gesture a covert invitation aimed at me? Is she asking me to come with her, in fact?

Norman No.

Tom Is she saying, I'm going to Hastings. If you care about me at all, you must come to Hastings?

Norman No.

Tom Having first, of course, told me, in so many words, by a series of hints exactly where she was going.

Norman Hastings.

Tom Yes.

Norman No. You've got the wrong end of the stick. If you want my opinion, that is subtle woman's language for stuff you, I'm off.

Tom No. I don't see that. I think I'll have to have it out with her.

Norman I wouldn't bother.

Tom I'm giving that cat up for today. Coming in?

Norman No, I'm going.

Tom Oh. I thought you said you were staying.

Norman No, I'm just passing through on my way to East Grinstead.

Tom Really? Business?

Norman Yes. International Association of Assistant Librarians Annual Conference.

Tom Jolly good.

Norman Exciting. (*Looking up in the tree*) Don't jump! Think of your
wife and kittens.

Tom Well, I'd better pop in.

Tom starts to move towards the house. Norman picks up his case

*Reg appears round the side of the house. He wears his cap and sports
jacket and carries two suitcases, and a bundle of magazines tied with
string*

Reg Oy—oy.

Tom Ah!

Norman Oh, no.

Reg Hallo, hallo. Who's this shifty-looking pair?

Tom Hallo there, Reg.

Reg Tom. (*He slaps him*) Norm. Surprised to see you. You're both looking
good. Both looking good.

Tom Yes—yes.

Reg What a day, eh? What a day. Ought to be knocking a ball about,
eh? Well, that little lot took us—(*he checks his watch*)—sixty-two
minutes exactly. Door to door. Forty-nine, nearly fifty miles as the
crow flies. Know the trick? There's a trick to it. Don't take the A two-
six-four. Take the A two-seven-two and then branch off on to the
B two-one-three-nine. It looks longer but it isn't.

Tom I usually take the A two-eight-one.

Norman Oh, my God.

Reg (*laughing*) How long does that take you?

Tom About an hour and a half.

Reg Door to door?

Tom Yes.

Reg Well, it would. You're going round the houses. If you want to go
that way, you'd do better to go through East Grinstead.

Norman (*jumping guiltily*) What, what?

Reg East Grinstead.

Norman Oh.

Tom Is Sarah here?

Reg Yes, yes. I think she went straight up to see Mother. (*Striding about*)
Well, look at this for a day. What about this sunshine? Just the ticket.
(*Spotting something in the tree*) Hallo, hallo. Anyone here a bird-watcher?

Norman Uh?

Reg Bird-watcher, are you? Like watching birds? (*He laughs*) What do
you make of that? Eh? You're a vet. What do you make of that?

Tom Yes.

Norman Good gracious, it's a cat.

Reg Cat. (*He laughs*) See it? Cat.

Tom Silly creature.

Reg Mother's cat, isn't it?

Tom Yes.

Reg Oh. Before I forget. Got another vet joke for you.

Tom Oh, yes.

Reg (*putting his arm round Tom's shoulders*) Question: what happens
when a vet walks through a deep puddle? Answer: he gets vater in his
vellingtons.

Tom Ha!

Reg Vater in his vellingtons! Heard that the other day. Tickled me.

Norman Ha!

Reg What brings you here today, Norman? I didn't expect to see you.
Ruth with you?

Norman No.

Reg Thank goodness for that. No offence, but thank goodness for that.

Tom He's passing through.

Norman Just passing through.

Reg Really?

Tom Going to East Grinstead.

Reg Ah, now. From here? You'll be going from here?

Norman Well, since this is where I am, it seems a good place to start.

Reg Turn left out of here—not right—through the village, then take the
right fork past the pub—brings you on to the A two-seven-two. Save
you ten miles.

Norman No, I don't fancy that way.

Reg Why not?

Norman I haven't got a car.

Reg Ah, well. Catch the bus.

Norman I'll do that.

Tom wanders to the house

Reg Where are you going?

Tom Just in.

Reg Try and persuade that wife of mine to put the kettle on.

Tom Ah.

Reg Ah!

Tom goes into the house

Norman How is she?

Reg Who?

Norman That wife of yours.

Reg I don't know. She's all right. When I last looked at her. (*He laughs*)
Well now, what's going on?

Norman Eh?

Reg She off with Tom? Our Annie? Going off for a sly one with Tom?

Norman Is she?

Reg Obvious. As soon as she wrote to Sarah—asked us to come and
look after Mother for the week-end—I thought, hallo, what's up.

Norman And Sarah?

Reg Sarah?

Norman What did she think?

Reg No idea. Didn't ask her. No, she's off with Tom. You could tell he was a bit on edge. Looked guilty. He must have been desperate.

Norman What do you mean, desperate?

Reg I mean. Knowing him. Not exactly one for taking the plunge, is he? Been hanging around here for, what, three years? And I bet you they haven't got further than a fumble on the sofa. Well, I'm glad. Glad for Annie. She's a bright girl. Not a great beauty but her heart's in the right place. Easy temperament, good around the house . . .

Norman All mod. cons., sunny view facing due south.

Reg What?

Norman You talk as if she's a property up for sale.

Reg No. No. All I'm saying . . .

Norman Better check her over for wood-worm while you're at it.

Reg (*laughing*) Check her over for wood-worm, I like that. (*Producing a bag from his pocket*) Want a toffee?

Norman Not at the moment.

Reg (*having one, the last in the bag*) What takes you to East Grinstead, then?

Norman Oh—business.

Reg Business?

Norman In a way.

Reg Oh, yes?

Norman (*winking*) Yes.

Reg (*laughing, knowingly*) Something lined up?

Norman You might say that.

Reg Bit of stuff?

Norman Just a little bit . . .

Reg Lucky chap. Hasn't got a friend, has she?

Norman She's got a sister but she's married.

Reg Oh, well. I'm not fussy. You're on.

Norman Reckon you'd get past Sarah?

Reg Ah. Well. Not seriously, no. (*He sits on the barrel*) I was only joking. I would never . . . Don't believe in that, personally. Mind you, I've been tempted. When you've been married a few years—you can't help window shopping. You know, the old urge. But you keep it under control, don't you? You have to. Well, *you* may not have to. But I have to. Not that there isn't something to be said for it. I've often thought it might actually help a marriage sometimes. It gets a bit stale, between you, you know. I'm not thinking just for me. For her, too. Sarah. I'm not being selfish. Perhaps if she—went off for a few days with someone— she might—well, it might make her a bit more—you know, give her a fresh—get her going again, for God's sake. If you follow me.

Norman Ah.

Reg Mind you, it'd never work for us. Sarah would never dream of going off. Pity. If she did, I could. But we're not like you and Ruth, you see.

Norman What are we like?

Reg Well—easier . . .

Norman There's nothing very easy about Ruth.

Reg No, I didn't mean easy like that, I meant—well, let's face it—you've always had, what shall we say—an unconventional relationship. Ruth was always a nonconformist, you know. Even when we were kids. I envy those types, sometimes. Mother was another, you know. In a different way. That old lady up there's had a life, I can tell you.

Norman I know.

Reg Wouldn't think so now. But she led our father a dance. Poor man really wasn't up to it. Shut himself in up there—pretended it all wasn't happening. Of course it was. Under his own roof sometimes. Well, it was bound to have an effect. Not so much on me—I was the eldest. Don't know what it did to Annie. She was younger. Think she just let it drift over her. Like she does now, most of the time. But Ruth. Ruth was altogether different.

Norman I know, I live with her.

Reg She took it—oddly.

Norman She's a mess.

Reg Putting it bluntly. She's got Mother's looks, mind you. Attractive, wouldn't you say? Difficult for a brother but—striking?

Norman Oh, yes.

Reg Annie and I always said she had our share, as well. Certainly had mine. I don't think Sarah married me for my looks.

Norman I wonder why she did.

Reg I don't know. That's a good question. I must ask her that sometime. (*He gets up*) Well, get going. She'll be looking for me. (*He picks up his suitcase*) Have a good trip. Think of me . . .

Norman I will.

Reg (*moving to the house, feeling the weight of his suitcase*) What the hell's she put in this one? Must have packed the bloody china cabinet. (*Turning back to Norman*) And another thing. We've got children. You haven't. That makes a difference. Can't go gallivanting off—not with children. Responsibilities. Blast it.

Sarah comes out from the house—smartly dressed in her summer best

Sarah Reg—oh. (*She sees Norman*) Hallo, Norman. (*She shakes his hand*)

Norman Hallo, Sarah. How's Sarah?

Sarah Very well, Norman. Surprised to hear you were here.

Norman Yes. Well, I was passing.

Sarah That's nice.

Norman Yes. Thought I'd look in on the old home.

Sarah Naturally.

Norman (*uneasy at her manner*) Well, I must be off. (*He gathers himself together and picks up his case, preparing to leave*)

Sarah Are you taking those in, Reg?

Reg Oh, yes. Yes . . . (*He starts to move in*)

Sarah I've just been talking to Annie.

Norman (*freezing in his tracks, warily*) Have you?

Sarah Yes. Oh, Reg, rather good news. She's decided she doesn't want to go away, after all.

Reg She doesn't?

Norman Eh?

Sarah No. Isn't that nice?

Reg Well, we needn't have bothered to come then.

Sarah I think it's just as well we did.

Reg (*going in*) All this racing about and we didn't need to come at all.

Reg goes inside

Sarah(*following him*) It gets difficult for her, coping entirely on her own ... (*Turning back and smiling brilliantly at Norman*) 'Bye, 'bye, Norman. I expect you'll want to hurry along to East Grinstead.

Sarah goes inside

Norman stands speechless with fury. He puts down his suitcase and paces up and down in silence for a second

Norman (*exploding with a fierce yell and kicking his suitcase frenziedly*) Damned—stupid—interfering—rotten—bitch!

Reg comes out to fetch the magazines he left behind

Reg Are you dashing off immediately or can you stay for a bit?

Norman I'm staying. You bet your sweet life I'm staying.

Norman snatches up his suitcase and strides angrily into the house. Reg, a little bewildered, follows him

CURTAIN

SCENE 2

The same. Saturday, 9 p.m.

Sarah and Reg come out from the house. They are supporting Norman who is very drunk

Sarah All right, put him here. Put him here ...

Reg (*lowering Norman on to the terrace steps*) Right. Down you come ...

Norman Thank you very much. Much obliged.

Reg Bit of fresh air should sober him up.

Sarah I have never known anyone who can ruin an evening as thoroughly as he can.

Norman Nobody loves me.

Sarah Norman . . .

Norman Nobody loves me at all.

Reg Shouldn't think so.

Sarah Norman! Norman, listen to me—will you stop feeling sorry for yourself. Anything that's happened to you is entirely your own fault.

Reg It's the fault of that home-made wine, if you ask me.

Sarah Reg . . .

Reg What?

Sarah Would you mind leaving us for a moment and doing something useful.

Reg What?

Sarah I don't know. Go and talk to Tom.

Reg Tom's gone home.

Sarah Well, you could wash up the supper things. That wouldn't hurt you for once.

Reg Annie's doing that, isn't she? She doesn't want me.

Sarah Annie is seeing to Mother. Anyway, we're supposed to be down here in order to give Annie a rest.

Reg We're supposed to have come down here in order that she can go away.

Sarah Well, she obviously isn't going away, is she? Not with this one.

Reg I don't know why you didn't let them instead of interfering.

Sarah Do you honestly believe it was me that stopped them going? Do you think I could have stopped them for a minute if they'd really wanted to go? If Annie had really wanted to go?

Reg I think you'd have had a good try. All right, I'll do the washing up.

Sarah And put an apron on first otherwise you'll ruin those trousers.

Reg You know, I wouldn't have missed this week-end for anything in the world . . .

Sarah fetches a cushion from the window-seat and sits by Norman

Reg goes in

Sarah Norman . . .

Norman Sarah, we're alone at last.

Sarah Norman.

Norman Mmm?

Sarah I think it's about time we had a talk.

Norman Oh, no—don't bother, honestly, Sarah. (*He puts his head in Sarah's lap*) I'll just curl up here in the garden. I won't be any more trouble, I promise you.

Sarah Norman.

Norman What?

Sarah Are you listening to me?

Norman Yes, yes . . .

Sarah I've no wish to waste my time with you if you're not going to listen to me. I've a dozen things I could be doing at home. I've got two children to worry about, a house, a husband—of sorts.

Norman puts his hand on Sarah's knee. Sarah gets up. Norman's head falls on the cushion. Sarah looks in the house, fetches a second cushion from the window-seat, closes the door, and sits by Norman

But the point is I seem to be the only one in this family capable of making any decision at all.

Norman lies straight, his head on the cushion

I mean, whether I like it or not, I seem to be the head of this family at the moment. By rights, it ought to be Reg—if you've lived with Reg, you know he can't even pay a gas bill. How he's still an estate agent after all these years I never cease to wonder. I'm amazed he hasn't sold someone the same house twice . . .

Norman What's wrong with that? That's standard estate agent's practice, isn't it?

Sarah Did you stop for a minute and seriously think of what you were doing when you asked Annie away this week-end? Did you ever think what the consequences might be?

Norman Ruth wouldn't care. She doesn't care.

Sarah I'm not worried about you and Ruth, your—well, what you do is your business—I'm thinking of Annie. What about her?

Norman She'd have had a good week-end. I'd have given her that. What have you ever given her? What's anyone ever given her?

Sarah Very noble of you . . .

Norman Not noble. She'd have probably given me a good week-end.

Sarah And what would have happened to her and Tom?

Norman He'd never have known.

Sarah He'd have found out.

Norman Meaning you would have told him?

Sarah No. Annie would have done.

Norman Annie? She's not that stupid . . .

Sarah She's in love with him.

Norman With Tom?

Sarah Yes.

Norman Rubbish. You've seen them together. She kicks him round the place like an old football. A punctured football. He doesn't even bounce back.

Sarah If she kicks him, it's probably the only way she can get any reaction from him at all. What else is a woman supposed to do if she's stuck with a man like that.

Norman Tom doesn't love anybody. Except cats and bull terriers—she's damn lucky he's so even tempered. I told him—the way she treats him —he ought to take a swing at her.

Sarah I'm sure she'd prefer that to being ignored.

Norman She doesn't want Tom . . . Stop trying to push everybody together, that cat's still up there. (*Calling*) Puss, puss, puss. He's gone now. You can come down . . . (*To Sarah*) Present company excepted, the trouble with the men in this house—and I include your husband—

is they allow themselves to be trampled on by the giant feet of their
cow elephant spouses.

Sarah Whose fault's that?

Norman Just because Reg happens to be a very gentle friendly soul—just
because Tom happens to be a man who's never had an aggressive
thought in his little head, in his little life, doesn't mean it's a cue for
every woman in sight to bounce up and down on them like nubile lady
trampoline artists—what have you done to him? Look at him, in there,
little Reg in his pinny, busy with his little bridget brush polishing away.
Polishing the plates for dear life because Sarah said so.

Sarah While you're lying out here stinking of drink.

Norman That's a man's role. To lie about stinking of drink.

Sarah I bet you've never washed up in your life.

Norman I line up the dishes and smash them—slowly—with the steak
tenderizer—remind me, I'll give Reg one for Christmas. That'd give
you something to complain about.

Sarah You really don't understand me at all, do you? You don't like me
and you've never tried to understand me . . .

Norman I understand you.

Sarah But you don't like me? Do you?

Norman I—don't dislike you. You make me irritable. You're like—mild
athlete's foot.

Sarah I see.

Norman I'll tell you. When I was at my primary school—mixed infants—
we had a little girl just like you. She was very pretty, very smart and clean
—beautifully dressed—always a nicely starched little frock on—nicely
ironed bow in her hair—butter wouldn't melt anywhere. Let alone her
mouth. And she ran that little school with more sheer ruthless efficiency
than the head of the Mafia. She asked you to do something for her and
you did it. You never argued. It was no good arguing with her. She was
cleverer than you were. Precociously clever. She could reduce a nine-
year-old thug to tears with her sarcasm. And it was no use trying to
thump her, either. She'd seduced all the best muscle in the place. She
had a body-guard five deep. Not that she ever needed it. For some reason,
she took a real dislike to me. Maybe because she could see what I really
thought of her. She made my life murder. I was terrified to go to school.
I used to pretend to be sick—I used to hide—play truant—anything rather
than go. And then one day, in the holidays, she came round with her
mother to our house to see my mother. A sociable tea and chat. And
they sent us two out on our own to play together. And suddenly there we
were, not in the school, not in the playground—which was definitely her
territory—but on mine. My garden, my patch. And we stood there and
we just looked at each other. And I thought what am I frightened of you
for? A skinny little girl with knock knees and a front tooth missing—
what on earth have I been frightened of you for, for heaven's sake?
(*Standing*) So I picked her up, like this under one arm and I carried her
right down the bottom of the garden by the rubbish tip—she never
made a sound during this, not a word, nothing—and I found the biggest

patch of stinging nettles I could find and I pulled down her knickers and sat her right in the middle of them. I felt marvellous. It was a beautiful moment. Magic. And she sat there for a very long time—not moving, just looking at me—weighing me up, you know. Then she got up, pulled up her knickers, very quietly took hold of my hand, gave me a big kiss and we went in and had our tea. I've never been in love like that again. (*He sits close to Sarah*)

Sarah I don't believe a word of that.

Norman It may have been an allegory.

Sarah Really? Meaning what?

Norman Meaning, watch it. This garden's full of nettles.

Sarah I believe you would, too. If you weren't so drunk.

Norman I would if I thought you'd give me a kiss . . . (*He reaches out and touches her hand*)

Sarah (*without moving her hand away*) Oh, Norman. Ruth, then Annie, then me. Be your age.

Norman (*taking her hand more firmly*) I don't mean any harm . . .

Sarah You're so dopey, I don't know how anybody could fall for you.

Norman God knows. (*He kisses her hand*) Animal magnetism.

Sarah You've no morals. No nothing, have you?

Norman I'm full of love.

Sarah And wine . . .

Norman (*moving closer*) By God, you're lovely.

Sarah (*snatching away her arm*) Now, Norman. That's enough . . .

Norman (*kneeling up by her*) Going to call Reg, are you?

Sarah (*remaining where she is*) That's enough . . .

Norman kisses her swiftly

Enough . . .

Norman (*softly*) Help, help, Reg . . .

Sarah That's enough, I said. (*She kisses him*) Quite enough—(*She kisses him*) No more . . .

Norman Sorry.

Sarah Enough. (*She kisses him again. This time it develops into a long kiss. Passionately*) Oh, my God, what am I doing . . .

Norman (*kissing her all over*) I know what you're doing. Don't worry. I'll tell you later.

Sarah (*struggling free*) Norman—Norman—I'll get you something to eat, Norman.

Norman (*persisting*) I've got you—that's enough . . .

Sarah (*still struggling*) No—please—Norman—please—let me get you something to eat—and then I'll come back . . . Norman. (*She pulls away finally and rises*)

Norman Where are you going, Sarah?

Sarah (*breathless*) I want to get you something to eat. I want you to eat something—please let me get you something to eat. I'll come back.

Norman Come back.

Sarah As soon as I've got you something . . .

Annie comes out of the house

A silence

Annie Oh, I'm sorry. Were you having a private conversation?
Sarah (*in some disarray*) No—no. I was just getting Norman something
to eat . . .

Sarah goes inside

Annie What's the matter with her?
Norman How do you mean?
Annie Well, she's all—jittery.
Norman No.
Annie Have you two been getting at each other again?
Norman Well—here and there.
Annie You've never got on with her, have you? I know she's difficult. I
mean, she drives me up the wall sometimes . . . but honestly, Norman,
if you can just try and be nice to her—it does pay off.
Norman I'll bear it in mind. (*He lies flat*)
Annie Look at you, you old tip . . . (*She kicks him*)
Norman Don't do that.
Annie Lovely night. I had to read to Mother. She wouldn't go off to sleep
for ages. I wouldn't mind but she likes these awful books.
Norman What sort? Horror stories, knowing her.
Annie They wouldn't be so bad. I don't object to horror stories. No, she
insists on all these torrid romances. I mean, really. It's bad enough
having to buy them, with their incredible front covers—I have to
wrap them round with copies of *Country Life* to carry them home. But
then having to read them out loud—it's awfully embarrassing. And
you can't skip anything. Come on, she says, come on they did more than
that, come on.
Norman She's an evil lady, that one. No wonder you're all peculiar.
Annie Norman.
Norman Uh?
Annie Look, I know why you got drunk tonight? (*She sits beside him*)
Norman Oh. You've guessed my secret.
Annie It was because I let you down, wasn't it?
Norman Good Lord, no.
Annie I feel really dreadful.
Norman Think nothing of it.
Annie The worst thing is, we planned the week-end in January—we
talked and wrote about it for six months—and you go ahead and get it
all organized and—well, I don't think I really could have gone, anyway.
It was just a dream. Something you think about but never really mean
to do. And then you turn up here and . . .
Norman The dream's shattered.
Annie What I'm saying is, don't blame Sarah. She merely said what I
was feeling. You mustn't take it out on her. You mustn't hate her.

Norman Right.

Annie It's my fault. I'm a coward.

Norman Forget it.

Annie Tom was awfully odd this evening. I don't think he knows, but I think he suspects. He was almost rude for Tom. Told me I looked like an old post office sack or something.

Norman Good God, the man's a sadist.

Annie I suppose I do a bit. I think I'm going to make one of my efforts tomorrow. I haven't made an effort for a bit.

Norman You're fine.

Annie Norman, look. I'm going to say something. But you're not to look at me while I'm saying it—do your promise?

Norman What do you intend to do while you're saying it, may I ask?

Annie Nothing. It's just I'll get embarrassed if you do . . .

Norman You're going to read me one of Mother's books, aren't you?

Annie Oh, Norman. This is frightfully difficult. Please . . .

Norman Sorry. Won't look.

Annie I promised you this week-end. I promised I'd go away with you and that I'd stay with you in a hotel and—everything. Well, I've let you down. I've been a coward.

Norman No, no . . .

Annie I think the bit that made me a coward was the going away bit, really. The actual thing of going into a hotel. All that pretending. It just isn't really me. I'd just get embarrassing and stupid.

Norman Never.

Annie Anyway. I'm not a coward about anything else . . . do you get what I mean?

Norman No.

Annie Oh, for heaven's sake . . . if you want to come to my room tonight, you'll be very welcome, that's all. You can look now.

Norman looks. A pause

Well?

Norman Well.

Annie I suppose I've done that all wrong, too.

Norman Not at all. Not at all.

A pause

Annie Well. Say something. Even if it's only thank you.

Norman Er—what time?

Annie What?

Norman Would you like me to come? What time would you like me to come?

Annie Well—when you like—I don't know. Don't make it too late, I'll be asleep.

Norman Right. It's just I've got one or two things to do first . . .

Annie Suit yourself. I'm going up to make up your bed. Just for appearances, I should get into it and make it look used. You know . . .

Norman Good point, yes.
Annie Just for Sarah's benefit.
Norman What?
Annie In case she . . .
Norman Yes, right. I'll mess it up for Sarah.
Annie Well . . .
Norman Well . . .
Annie See you later then?
Norman Right.

Annie kisses Norman

Reg appears in an apron holding a salad basket

Reg (*seeing them*) Oh. Beg your pardon, beg your pardon . . .
Annie What for?
Reg (*winking*) Sorry, sorry. I saw nothing. Nothing at all. Don't worry.
   (*Holding up the salad basket*) Sarah says, where does this go?
Annie I don't know. Just sling it on top of the cupboard. That's what I
   do.
Reg Oh, right . . .
Annie (*taking it from him*) It's all right. I'll do it, I'm going in. Anyway,
   you've got to know how to sling it . . .

Annie goes indoors

Reg Hallo there, Norman.
Norman Hallo there, Reg. You come to seduce me?
Reg Eh?
Norman Nothing.
Reg Ah. That's done that, anyway. I hate washing up. Look at these
   hands. Ruined. (*He laughs*) Hey, I'm going to get myself a drink. Do
   you want one?
Norman Great.
Reg Think we've earned one.
Norman Bring the bottle.
Reg Right.

Reg goes in

Norman This boy can do no wrong tonight. He has the Midas touch.
   Every woman turns to gold. (*Shouting at the cat*) Come down here, cat.
   You don't know what you're missing.

Reg reappears with a bottle and two glasses

Reg Who are you shouting at?

Norman points

Oh, yes. Hallo, pussy. Here we are. The last of mother's home-made parsnip.

Norman takes the bottle from him. Reg holds out two glasses. Norman fills one and wanders away with the bottle

Don't you want a glass?

Norman I'll drink from the bottle. I'm all man tonight.

Reg (*sitting on the barrel*) Wish I was. I'm clapped out. Cheers. (*He drinks*)

Norman Good health, Reg. (*He swigs*) Ah, it's a good night, Reg. It's a lovely night.

Reg Beautiful . . .

Norman It's on a night such as this that all the old base instincts of primitive man, the hunter, come flooding up. You long to be away— free—filled with the urge to rape and pillage and conquer.

Reg I've just got the urge to put my feet up. I think my ankles are swelling again. (*He rolls up his trouser-legs and takes off his shoes and one sock*)

Norman My God! I'm filled with the lust for conquest tonight.

Reg (*examining his legs*) I'm going to get varicose veins if I'm not careful. That'll be the next thing. I've just about got everything else . . .

Norman (*excitedly*) Reg, I have this tremendous idea. I want to tell you about this tremendous idea, Reg. May I tell you about my tremendous idea?

Reg All right, yes, if you want to . . .

Norman It's suddenly come to me, this tremendous idea. It's terrific. Let's all of us—you, me, Tom—let's take a couple of weeks and just go . . .

Reg Go? Where?

Norman Anywhere. Just we men . . .

Reg Do you mean a holiday?

Norman Well, in a way—no, not a holiday—that sounds so damn conventional. I want us just to go. And see things. And taste things. And smell things. And touch things—touch trees—and grass—and—and earth. Let's touch earth together, Reg.

Reg Where were you thinking of going?

Norman Everywhere. Let's see everywhere. Let's be able to say—we have seen and experienced everything.

Reg We'd have to be going some to do that in two weeks, wouldn't we?

Norman I've never really looked before, you know, Reg. These kids today, you know, they've got the right ideas. This world is my world and I'm going to wrap my arms right round it and hug it to me.

Reg I'd go easy on that stuff, you know . . .

Norman In one great big bloody beautiful embrace.

Reg Yes. Ssh, now quietly, Norman. Mother's asleep.

Norman When you think of the things we've done with our lives—our little lives up to this moment—you realize—what a waste. What a dreadful waste. (*To the heavens*) Please don't let me die till I've seen it. Please don't let me die.

Reg (*rising anxiously*) It's all right, Norman. You're not going to die, it's all right.

Norman (*turning and embracing Reg*) Oh, Reg . . .

Reg Ssh. Steady on. Steady on. Quietly . . .

Norman (*tearfully*) You're my brother, Reg, my brother.

Reg Yes, well, brother-in-law, yes. (*He tries to disentangle himself*) Look, Norman . . .

Norman Let's stop hating and start to love, Reg.

Reg Ssh. Yes, yes—good idea . . .

Norman I love you, Reg. I'm not ashamed to say that to my brother. I love you.

Reg That's good news, Norman, yes.

Sarah enters with a plate of sandwiches. She stops as she sees the men Annie, alarmed by the noise, enters separately behind her, pillow-case in hand

Norman I love you, Reg, I love you.

Norman collapses clasping Reg's knees. Reg looks at the women. Annie and Sarah look at each other, then back at Reg

Reg He's—er—he's obviously had a—he's had a—he's . . . (*He pauses*)

Sarah We'd better get him inside.

Reg Yes.

Sarah puts down her plate. They gather round Norman preparing to drag him inside. Norman starts sobbing

He's crying.

Sarah He's drunk. That's all he is, drunk. Come on, we'll have to pull him. I'm not lifting him. Come on—pull . . .

Reg starts to haul Norman into the house

Norman (*as he goes; tearfully, to Sarah*) Nobody loves me. (*To Annie*) Nobody loves me . . .

Reg hauls Norman into the house. Sarah picks up Reg's shoes and follows. Annie picks up the sandwiches and cushions and goes in after Sarah: she looks out of the window, then disappears

CURTAIN

ACT II

Scene 1

The same. Sunday, 11 a.m.

Ruth is standing thoughtfully. Sarah is moving around with an insecticide spray, spraying the roses. Two slightly ancient collapsible garden chairs are leaning against the barrel

Ruth Well.

Sarah Yes.

Ruth Norman and Annie. Well, well.

Sarah Yes. I thought you ought to know.

Ruth Thank you for phoning me. I don't know what I'm expected to do, though.

Sarah Well . . .

Ruth I mean, one can't take it very seriously. It's obviously only another of Norman's gestures against the world or whatever. It's not as if they've even done anything.

Sarah I think you might've done a little more than just laugh. I mean, if I'd been in your position I certainly would have . . .

Ruth Sarah, dear, I've been married to Norman for five years. I have learnt through bitter experience that the last thing to do with Norman is to take him seriously. That's exactly what he wants. I'm not saying it isn't a strain sometimes to keep smiling when he's behaving particularly bizarrely and threatening to burn down the house. When he really gets on top of me, I just go to bed and lock the door.

Sarah I'm amazed you've stayed with him, I really am.

Ruth Well, I don't really look at it that way. I rather think of him as staying with me. After all, I make all the payments on the house, most of the furniture is mine. It has crossed my mind, in moments of extreme provocation, to throw him out—but I don't know, I think I must be rather fond of him. It's a bit like owning an oversized unmanageable dog, being married to Norman. He's not very well house-trained, he needs continual exercising—mental and physical—and it's sensible to lock him up if you have visitors. Otherwise he mauls them. But I'd hate to get rid of him.

Sarah That's all very well if you keep him under proper control. When he goes upsetting other people's lives. Annie's, for example . . .

Ruth You really can't blame Norman entirely, you know. He only jumps up at people who encourage him. It's a general rule, if you don't want him licking your face, don't offer him little titbits. I don't mean just Annie either.

Sarah I don't know what you're talking about.

Ruth Oh, come on, Sarah, I'm sure at some time he's cast an eye in your
   direction.

Sarah Certainly not.

Ruth In fact I've seen him do it.

Sarah Rubbish. Don't assume everyone's motives are the same as your
   own. Anyway, the point is, so far as I can gather, Annie and Tom are
   practically not on speaking terms. They had words, apparently, last
   night. I don't think he knows about Norman, but all the same, Tom
   senses something. He's very upset.

Ruth Oh, she's not still with that limp man . . .

Sarah Tom would make her a very good husband. I mean, he may have
   his faults but when you compare him to some men—he's kind, very
   considerate. He's done a lot for Annie over the years . . .

Ruth He's as selfish as hell.

Sarah That is just not true . . .

Ruth He is quite content, from all accounts, to come round here day
   after day, eat her food, use the place as a second home—come and go
   just as he pleases and what's he given her in return? Absolutely nothing.

Sarah I think that's extremely unfair.

Ruth He's a parasite. Like one of the tics on his wretched animals.

Sarah Oh well, it's obviously not worth discussing this with you. We don't
   see eye to eye on anything. We never have.

Ruth (*taking one of the chairs and starting to put it up*) Quite right. Very
   sensible. I'm going to enjoy a bit of sun. Then I'm going home to do
   some work. It was very kind of you to phone me and express so much
   concern over my relationship with Norman. As I say, there's nothing I
   can do about it, Norman is a law unto himself and always has been
   and I have a mountain of work to do by tomorrow—what the hell's
   wrong with this chair? (*She struggles to put it up*)

Sarah If you'd wear your glasses it would help.

Ruth Oh, don't you start on me about my glasses. Norman's bad enough.

Sarah You grope about—drive cars . . .

Ruth Look, go away, Sarah. You're a pain in the neck.

Sarah I think Norman's just about what you deserve, I really do . . .

Ruth (*still grappling*) Damn and blast this thing . . .

Sarah Here, come on, let me . . .

Ruth (*fiercely*) Oh, go away.

Sarah All right, all right. I still don't know why you won't wear your
   glasses. They're a great improvement.

   Sarah goes into the house

*Ruth glares after her. She has one final go at the chair, then finally perches
on it uncomfortably, upright, still unopened*

   Tom wanders on by the statue

Tom Oh. Ruth. Hallo.

Ruth Who's that?

Tom goes near enough for her to see who it is

Oh—hallo.
Tom You're here?
Ruth Yes.
Tom Ah.

Tom notices the way Ruth is sitting on her chair. He studies her for a moment, puzzled

Er . . .
Ruth What?
Tom Nothing. I—er . . . (*Gesturing vaguely towards her chair*) Nothing.

Tom selects the other chair, is about to put it up then decides, perhaps out of courtesy, to sit on it the same as Ruth is doing on hers

Seen Norman?
Ruth Yes.
Tom Ah. Seen Annie?
Ruth Yes.
Tom Ah.

A pause

Ruth I've also seen Reg and Sarah—in fact, I think I've seen just about everybody there is to see.
Tom Ah. Now you've seen me.
Ruth Yes. I've seen you.
Tom You look—different. Can't think why. Different.
Ruth I'm older, perhaps.
Tom No, no—can't think. It'll come to me. (*A pause*) Er . . .
Ruth What?
Tom I was just wondering if there was any reason why we were sitting like this.
Ruth I don't know why you should be.
Tom No, nor do I.
Ruth I know why I am.
Tom Oh? Why?
Ruth Because I can't put the bloody thing up.
Tom (*leaping into action*) Oh. Well. Just a sec. Excuse me. Hang on. (*He puts the chair up*) Here we are.
Ruth Thank you.

They both sit, Tom on his chair still unopened

Tom You've seen Annie, you say?
Ruth Yes.
Tom Ah. How did she look?
Ruth Aren't you going to put your chair up?
Tom Oh, yes. Good idea.

Tom puts up his chair and sits

Ruth Annie looks very well. From what I've seen.

Tom The point is—I think I'm in her bad books.

Ruth Really?

Tom Yes. I rather went at her last night. Tore her off a strip.

Ruth You did?

Tom Yes, I thought it might—well, she seemed to be taking me far too much for granted.

Ruth Was she?

Tom So I thought a couple of sharp words might do the trick. I told her to straighten herself up.

Ruth Did you?

Tom Told her she looked a mess.

Ruth Really.

Tom Yes. I threatened to belt her. Really let rip.

Ruth I see.

Tom I haven't slept a wink. Do you think I've damaged my chances?

Ruth Chances of what?

Tom I don't know. Just general chances.

Ruth Well. Some women do respond awfully well to that sort of treatment. They enjoy tremendously being told they look a mess—and they actually thrill to the threat of physical violence. I've never met one that does, mind you, but they probably do exist. In books. By men. But then, there are probably some women who enjoy being thrown into canals. One just doesn't bump into them every day—not even in this family.

Tom You reckon I might possibly have been on the wrong track?

Ruth I'd have thought so.

Tom Oh, well. For once he was wrong.

Ruth Who was wrong?

Tom Norman.

Ruth Norman? Did Norman tell you to do that?

Tom He suggested I do something of the sort.

Ruth Insult her and threaten to beat her up?

Tom Yes. He's generally right. About women, anyway. He's got a good instinct, has Norman. Has a way with women. I shouldn't really be saying this, should I?

Ruth (*after looking at Tom for a while incredulously*) Tom.

Tom Um?

Ruth At the risk of pouring bad advice on bad, I think perhaps I ought to point you in the right direction.

Tom Do. Yes, do. Any advice . . .

Ruth Firstly, there are fallacies in Norman's well-known universal theory of womanhood with which, as it happens as his wife, I am familiar. He claims that women can be divided into two groups—the ones you stroke and the ones you swipe. There has been some research done on this and it's been discovered quite recently that they are actually a little more complex.

Tom Yes, yes. It follows . . .

Ruth Good. They enjoy flattery no less than a man does. Though if you are flattering a woman, it pays to be a little more subtle. You don't have to bother with men, they believe any compliment automatically . . .

Tom Oh, come on. Hardly, hardly . . .

Ruth Well, we won't argue that. All I'm saying is, Tom, you're an intelligent man, you're not unattractive . . .

Tom Oh well, thank you very much.

Ruth And you obviously feel a lot of things that you don't show—necessarily. Which is marvellous in a crisis but a bit disheartening in times of peace.

Tom How do you mean?

Ruth I think you have to give a little. Give, Tom, do you see?

Tom Ah.

Ruth Do you follow me?

Tom (*comprehending*) Aha—yes. (*He sits back and ponders this*) Give a little what?

Ruth Oh, my God. (*Impatiently*) You're a very frustrating person to talk to, Tom. I feel like a tame mouse on one of those wheels they have in cages—one keeps running round and round like mad getting nowhere.

Tom That's interesting you should mention that. There have been some studies done. Mice and wheels and it's really quite remarkable. One of the things they discovered . . .

Ruth Yes, right. Thank you.

Tom Eh?

Ruth Don't let's wander off the subject.

Tom No.

Ruth (*studying him*) I think your brain works all right. I think what must happen is, it receives a message from the outside—but once that message gets inside your head, it must be like an unfiled internal memo in some vast Civil Service department. It gets shunted from desk to desk with nobody willing to take responsibility for it. Let's try some simple reactions, shall we? I hate you, Tom. Do you hear? I hate you.

Tom Um?

Ruth Oh well, try again. I love you, Tom. I love you.

Tom (*laughing nervously*) I don't quite get this—a game, is it?

Ruth No, Tom, it is not a game. It's an attempt to communicate.

Tom Ah.

Ruth You're refreshing after Norman, I'll give you that. Who is never one to hide anything. He has three emotions for every occasion.

Tom I know what it is. Why you look different. You're not wearing your glasses.

Ruth No.

Tom Makes a great difference to you, that. Without your glasses.

Ruth Thank you, Tom. That's good. You're learning.

Tom I think I prefer you with them on, actually. It gives your face a better shape. (*Gesturing vaguely*) Sort of . . .

Ruth (*menacing*) Tom . . .

Tom Um?

Ruth Do you get on well with your animals, by any chance?

Tom Yes, yes, generally . . .

Ruth You amaze me. You have a disastrous effect on me, did you know that?

Tom Oh.

Ruth Everything tends to boil over ever so slightly.

Tom Oh. It's pretty warm.

Ruth I have a desire to put on my glasses and take off my clothes and dance naked on the grass for you, Tom. I'd put on my glasses not in order to improve the shape of my face, but in order to see your reaction, if any. And as I whirled faster and faster—the sun glinting on my lenses —flashing messages of passion and desire, I would hurl you to the ground, rip off your clothes and we would roll over and over making mad, torrid, steaming love together. How does that grab you, Tom?

Tom (*after a moment*) Good Lord. (*He laughs*) Have to be careful where you rolled on this grass.

Ruth Oh. (*She sits back exhausted, head in hands*)

Tom (*watching her anxiously*) Ruth? Are you all right? Fairly hot this sun. Nearly overhead. (*Rising*) Perhaps you ought to have a lie down . . .

Ruth I'm sorry. I'm exhausted. I've done my best. I'm sorry.

Tom (*flapping round her*) Can I get you an aspirin?

Ruth lies back with her eyes closed. Tom moves anxiously back to his chair and sits

Look, I had no idea you felt like this. I honestly had no idea.

Ruth Like what?

Tom Like that. With me.

Ruth (*through gritted teeth*) I have never hidden my feelings towards you, Tom.

Tom I had no idea . . .

Ruth What are you talking about, Tom?

Tom I feel terrible about this. Absolutely terrible. This has complicated things no end. I mean, it looks as if the ball's in my court rather. Yes, you've bowled me a googly there.

Ruth What the hell is a googly?

Tom If a woman, unexpectedly, suddenly tells you she loves you, where do you go from there?

Ruth Are we talking theoretically?

Tom If you like.

Ruth Well, it's rather up to you then, isn't it? Firstly, you have to ask yourself, do I love her.

Tom Well, I haven't had much time to think. I mean, love's a bit strong. Anyway, there's somebody else.

Ruth What are you talking about?

Tom Well, there's Norman. I've got to think of Norman's feelings.

Ruth Norman? Don't be so damned ridiculous. As far as Norman's concerned, this is some passing romantic pipe-dream. So stop using Norman

as an excuse for your own inadequacy. If you don't grab quickly, somebody else will sooner or later. Someone with a little more determination
than Norman ever had.

Tom Well, I'm sorry. That's all I can say. I had no idea. Does Norman
know, do you think?

Ruth What?

Tom About me?

Ruth Of course he knows.

Tom Oh, that explains it. That's why he's been a bit odd towards me.
Slightly strained, you know. (*He rises and wanders, ending up behind his
chair*) Oh well. (*A pause*) You're looking very nice, by the way. Lovely.
Very nice indeed. Very well turned out.

Ruth I think you're a raving lunatic.

Tom (*modestly*) Well, I go a bit over the moon, sometimes. You don't
need to worry.

*Annie comes out. She has made her effort. She has done her hair, made up
a little and has a dress on*

Tom Oh, hallo.

Annie Hallo. You both want some coffee out here?

Tom Oh, well . . .

Ruth (*getting up*) No. I've had enough sun. I think I'll go and brave
Mother. (*She goes towards the house, leaving her handbag*)

Annie Yes, she's awake. I've just been in with her.

Ruth Right. (*Passing close to Tom*) Talk to her.

Tom Eh?

Ruth Tell her.

Tom Oh.

Annie You want coffee, Tom?

Tom No, that's all right. (*Studying Annie*) You know, you look different
somehow. What is it?

Ruth (*as she goes*) She probably hasn't got her glasses on.

Ruth goes in

Tom No. It isn't that. It'll come to me.

Annie Don't force it.

A pause

Did you catch the cat?

Tom Yes. He was round the front there, when I arrived. Sitting in the
sun, purring away.

Annie Good. Is his paw better?

Tom Oh, yes. It wasn't anything serious really—I . . .

Annie The way you went on about it, I thought you were going to have
to amputate a leg.

Tom No, well—actually, you may not have noticed but you probably
seem to have the unhealthiest cat in the country.

Annie He hasn't had a day without something. He's either got feeble
resistance or else he's a terrific hypochondriac. I don't know which.
It's the only cat I know with a personal physician.

Tom I'm afraid I do rather use him actually. As a reason for coming.

Annie Well, there's no need. You're welcome any time. It seems a bit
unfair to keep pumping him full of medicine, just as an excuse for a
meal.

Tom I don't quite do that . . .

Annie Well . . .

Tom Yes.

Annie Any time.

Tom Thanks.

A pause

Annie Tom. I've got to tell you something. (*She sits in one of the chairs*)

Tom Yes. So have I. (*He sits in the other chair*)

Annie Yes, well let me tell you mine first. I think I know what you're
going to say and this may make all the difference. The point is that this
week-end Norman asked me to go away with him.

Tom Norman?

Annie Yes. He wanted us to go away together for a week-end. As you
see we didn't go, but—I thought you ought to know that we were
considering it. I nearly agreed. There, I've said it. That's it.

Tom (*slowly*) I see.

Annie I'm sorry.

Tom No—no . . .

Annie Are you hurt?

Tom Well—I understand—I think . . .

Annie You do? You wouldn't have wanted me to go, would you?

Tom No. But I don't think I'd have had the right to stop you.

Annie Yes, well, maybe not—technically. I know we're not that close. All
the same, I thought you might have felt . . .

Tom No, it's not that. It's not you. It's just that I think I understand
what Norman was doing.

Annie He was asking me away to a hotel.

Tom Yes, I know that. But why was he?

Annie Why does any man?

Tom Yes, yes, yes. But you see, behind all that, in some obscure way, I
think he wanted to get back at me.

Annie Get back at you?

Tom He knows, you see.

Annie Knows what?

Tom About Ruth and me.

Annie Ruth and you?

Tom Yes. That's what I wanted to tell you.

Annie You and Ruth?

Tom Yes.

Annie But you haven't—with Ruth . . . ?

Tom No. Not *with* Ruth, no.

Annie Well, with who, then?

Tom No, it is with Ruth but not me with Ruth, rather Ruth with me. There's a difference.

Annie Is there?

Tom Yes. You see, it appears that Ruth—you'll have to bear with me, this is fraught with embarrassment—Ruth, you see—I'm so useless at this, I never pick up these signals and signs and hints till it's far too late. Ruth's apparently been carrying a torch for me.

Annie She has?

Tom I didn't encourage her, I promise you. As a matter of fact, I didn't even know. 'Till just now.

Annie Are you sure you've got this right, Tom? Ruth can be a little— well, quick, you know. I mean, I'm not saying you did, but could you have missed the point?

Tom No. I assure you, I did not miss the point. No chance of that. Rather wish I had. She made it all graphically clear. She wanted to take off her clothes—oh, well it's very embarrassing. I won't go into it.

Annie No, go on. Take off her clothes?

Tom Oh, well she went on, you know. I hate you, I love you—I want to roll about naked in my glasses . . .

Annie Are you sure you got this right?

Tom Yes. She said she'd never belonged to Norman. It was just a pipe-dream—that Norman knew all about it and I'd better grab her while she's still boiling over.

Annie I don't believe it. What did you say?

Tom I was a bit taken aback. I said I'd have to think it over.

Annie (*indignant*) Think it over?

Tom Obviously.

Annie What about me?

Tom Yes, well, that too . . .

Annie Yes, that too . . .

Tom Oh, goodness, this is getting awfully difficult.

Annie Not at all. It's not difficult. Don't let me stand in your way. You rush off.

Tom No—no . . .

Annie Go on. Go on. Good riddance.

Tom No, Annie, I . . .

Annie And in future I'd be grateful if you'd stop molesting our damn cat.

Reg appears in shirt sleeves. He has a tennis ball with him

Reg Right! Here we are. I've got the ball. Catch, Annie . . .

He pretends to throw the ball to Annie

Annie Oh, Reg, not now . . .

Reg Come on. Come on. (*Calling indoors*) Norman! Come on out. We can all do with some exercise. Stuck indoors far too much.

Annie Reg, please, not just at the . . .

Norman comes out. He wears shorts and a tee shirt

Norman Right, where's the action then?
Reg What are you wearing?
Norman Found them upstairs in the cupboard.
Reg I think they're my old ones.
Norman Thank you for the loan. (*Seeing Annie*) Hey-hey! What is this,
   I see?
Annie What?
Norman Look at her. Just take a look at this beautiful girl.
Reg Oh, yes. She's got a skirt on.
Norman The sunshine has brought the butterfly out of its chrysalis. Isn't
   she beautiful? (*He pretends to faint*)
Annie All right, Norman, don't overdo it.
Norman No, honestly, you look great. Doesn't she, Tom?
Tom That's what it is. You've got a thing on. A dress. I knew there was
   something different.
Norman Give the boy a wolf cub badge. (*To Annie*) Fantastic.
Annie Oh, shut up.
Reg Are we going to play a game?
Norman Right.
Annie No.
Norman Oh, come on. Don't get ladylike just because you're in drag.
Reg What are you playing?
Norman I know. I've got it. Strip catch. Every time you drop the ball, you
   take something off. Here, Annie, catch. (*He mimes throwing the ball
   to her. Annie reacts*) Missed. Right, get 'em off.
Annie Norman, I'll thump you.
Reg Right. I've got it. Listen. The person with the ball—he calls out
   somebody's name. And at the same time, he must throw the ball to
   somebody else. He mustn't throw it to the person whose name he's
   called out. And he mustn't call his own name. Otherwise, he loses a life.
   Two lives. And you lose a life if you drop it. Right, here we go. Catch,
   Tom.

Reg throws the ball to Annie

Tom (*reacting*) What?
Annie (*catching the ball*) Oh. (*She hesitates*)
Reg Keep it going. You must keep it going fast.
Annie Right. Er—Reg.

Annie throws the ball to Norman

Norman Annie.

Norman throws to Tom

Tom Ah. Norman.

Tom throws to Annie

Annie Norman.

Annie throws to Tom

Tom Tom. Oh, no, that's me. Sorry.
Reg Right, that's one life gone.
Tom Sorry—er—Reg.

Tom throws to Annie

Annie Tom.

Annie throws to Norman

Norman Annie.

Norman throws to Reg. Reg drops it

Reg Not too hard. Right, that's one life for me. Annie.

Reg throws to Norman

Norman Annie.

Norman throws to Tom

Tom Annie.

Tom throws to Annie

　　Oh—sorry . . .
Reg Out! Right, Tom's out.
Tom Sorry. I'm no good at this sort of thing. I'll watch. (*He sits*)
Reg Annie, come on.
Annie Norman.

Annie throws to Reg

Reg Annie.

Reg throws to Norman

Norman Catch it, Reg.

Norman throws to Annie. Annie drops it

Norman (*triumphant*) Ha-ha!

Reg laughs. Annie looks annoyed

Annie Norman.

Annie throws to Reg, who drops it

Reg Steady on, steady on, I wasn't ready.
Norman You were ready, you're out.
Reg No, I wasn't. I wasn't ready. (*To Tom*) You were watching. I wasn't
　　ready, was I?

Tom Sorry, I missed that.
Norman You're out.
Reg Rubbish
Annie What happens now?
Norman Just us two.
Reg You can't play with just two of you.
Norman Yes, we can.
Reg Don't be daft—I mean . . .
Norman (*throwing the ball to Annie*) Annie.
Annie Norman. (*She throws to him*) This is stupid.
Norman Annie. (*He throws to Annie*) No, it isn't.
Reg Oh well, let 'em play if they want to. (*He sits by Tom*)

*Under the ensuing conversation, Norman and Annie continue their game—
calling each other's name, getting closer together until they are throwing the
ball a few inches distance and finally passing it hand to hand*

Reg How's that car of yours running?
Tom Oh, no complaints. No complaints.
Reg It's funny because my next-door neighbour, he's bought one of those.
Same year—same model as yours—he's had a lot of bad luck with his.
Tom Has he?
Reg He'd done—what?—eight hundred miles, barely run it in. He's
starting up this fairly steep hill—in fourth—he changes to third—big
lorry behind him, big lorry—front of him—finds he needs to change to
second and whack—whole gear lever comes off in his hand. There he is,
on this steep hill, stuck in third gear, just about to stall—lorry there—
lorry there—could have been nasty.
Tom Good Lord.

*Annie and Norman, unseen by them, are now on the ground locked in an
embrace*

Reg As it happens, luckily, he has the presence of mind to turn his wheel
off the road into the ditch.

*Ruth comes out to collect her handbag which she has left by the chair.
She goes towards Norman and Annie—then peers at them, during the
following*

Safest place. What else could he do? He said, that's the last time I buy
one of those. You won't catch me buying one of those again. You've
been lucky up till now, that's all I can say.
Ruth (*who has been peering at the shape of Norman and Annie on the ground
for some seconds*) Excuse me, I'm sorry to interrupt, but could you just
confirm that I'm seeing what I think I'm seeing?

Reg and Tom turn

Reg Flipping heck.
Tom (*rising*) Hey! Hey! (*Moving to Norman and Annie*) Annie—Annie . . .

Annie (*emerging for a second*) Oh, go away.

Ruth Well, throw a bucket of water over them or something.

Tom Annie! (*Angry for him*) All right. Two can play at that. Two can play at that. (*He marches up to Ruth*) I love you, too. Do you hear, I love you, too.

Ruth I beg your pardon.

Tom I love you. (*He grabs Ruth and kisses her*)

Ruth (*struggling furiously*) Tom . . .

Reg stands between the couples, greatly amused

Sarah comes out with a tray

Sarah Now, I'm collecting dirty cups. Are there any . . . Oh, my God. Tom! Tom! Ruth! Norman! Annie! What are you . . . ? Stop them. Somebody stop them. Reg . . .

Reg stands uselessly laughing

Reg, will you do something for once in your life?

Curtain

Scene 2

The same. Monday, 9 a.m.

Ruth enters, ready to leave. She takes one of the chairs and places it level with the barrel. Sarah enters, also dressed ready to go.

Sarah Look at the time. We should be half-way home by now.

Ruth Sorry to hold you up. (*She sits*)

Sarah It gives you a lot of trouble, does it? Your car?

Ruth Now and then. It sometimes starts all right. But only if you're not in a hurry to go anywhere.

Sarah (*fetching the second chair and placing it near Ruth*) Reg'll get it going.

Ruth I hope so.

Sarah It's nice Tom came back this morning. (*She sits*)

Ruth Yes.

Sarah I'm glad he didn't decide to go off in a huff.

Ruth No.

Sarah After yesterday. He could have done.

Ruth He has a forgiving nature.

Sarah Yes. But then I suppose one could say that of you.

Ruth That's one of the hazards of living with Norman. It was much more alarming being attacked by Tom. That I wasn't even expecting.

Reg enters from the tennis court, jacket off, sleeves up, wiping his hands on a rag

Reg Fuse wire. We need a bit of fuse wire.
Sarah Look at your hands.
Reg Well, I've been . . .
Sarah For heaven's sake, don't get it on your shirt.
Reg (*to Ruth*) It's a very dirty engine you've got there. (*He sits on the barrel*)
Ruth Sorry. We seldom get round to washing that.
Reg Let alone the outside.
Ruth It's very kind of you.
Reg No trouble. What I'll do is, I'll bind it on with a bit of fuse wire. It'll only be temporary but it should get you home. She'll still need a shove to start. Could you get it for me?
Sarah What?
Reg Fuse wire.
Sarah Why can't you get it?
Reg Well, look at my hands. I'll get it all over everything.
Sarah Well, I don't see why I . . .
Reg All right, I'll get it myself. I'll only open the door with my teeth.
Sarah (*rising*) Oh, I'll get it then. As usual. What is it you want?
Reg Fuse wire. It's usually in the bottom kitchen drawer. That's where we used to keep it. It's very thin, silver-coloured wire wrapped round a . . .
Sarah I know what fuse wire looks like.
Reg Fine.
Sarah Wait there. I don't know.

Sarah goes into the house

Reg Soon have it fixed.
Ruth Thank you.
Reg I hope so, anyway. We have to get underway soon or she'll be complaining again. I don't know why we're in such a hurry to get home. I don't have to collect the children till this afternoon. Could have enjoyed the sun. You ought to be at work too, oughtn't you?
Ruth I think I've just taken the day off. So has Norman.
Reg Ah well, why not.
Ruth Sarah's being almost amiable towards me at the moment. I don't know why that should be, do you?
Reg No . . .
Ruth I'm afraid I suspect her when she's nice to me. I don't want to sound mean about your wife but whenever she smiles it usually means some disaster is about to overtake me. She was extremely cheerful on my wedding day, I seem to remember.
Reg Ah.
Ruth What's she up to? Do you know?
Reg Well . . .

Ruth What?

Reg (*moving to sit in Sarah's chair*) It's silly but—er—this sounds ridiculous —but do you think Norman has—er . . .

Ruth Has what?

Reg Well—you know. Towards Sarah . . .

Ruth Norman and Sarah?

Reg No, I don't think he can, but—I just has this idea. I think I'm just getting jumpy. He's been round everyone else, hasn't he?

Ruth Everyone else being Annie.

Reg Well, yes. If you like.

Ruth I don't think you should suspect Norman of everything, you know.

Reg No, no—I just . . .

Ruth He can't be held responsible for every strange relationship in this family.

Reg No. I'm sorry. I just . . .

Ruth He's not a complete monster.

Reg No. (*He gets up*)

Sarah enters with a roll of gardening wire

Ah.

Sarah There's none there. Only this. (*She sits in the chair*)

Reg That's garden wire.

Sarah I know it's garden wire. This is all there is.

Reg Worse than useless. Much too thick.

Sarah Well, I'm trying to help.

Reg We need fuse wire. I'll find it, don't worry.

Sarah I've just said there isn't any.

Reg Of course there is. I'll find it.

Sarah You won't you know.

Reg Want a bet?

Sarah Why do you always want to make me out a liar?

Reg You missed it. It's there.

Sarah (*rising*) All right, I'll show you. It isn't there.

Reg and Sarah move towards the house

Reg It's there.

Sarah It is not there.

Reg It's always there.

Reg and Sarah go into the house

Ruth continues to sit

Norman enters from the tennis court

Norman Where's the man with the fuse wire then?

Ruth Arguing with his wife, surprisingly. They can't find it.

Norman Oh.
Ruth Would that have anything to do with you?
Norman Me? I haven't got the fuse wire.
Ruth I mean, them arguing.
Norman (*sitting in the chair*) Glad we're staying at home today.
Ruth I don't think my office will be, particularly
Norman We'll have a great time. Let's do something fun.
Ruth We could wash up.
Norman No.
Ruth There's about two months' worth.
Norman No. That's not fun.
Ruth You could cut our hedge. That man next door complained again.
   He said he's writing to the council.
Norman Stupid git. Why doesn't he move.
Ruth That's what he said about us.
Norman It's very cruel to cut hedges. Tell him it's against my principles.
Ruth You tell him. So you haven't been making eyes at Sarah?
Norman Sarah?
Ruth In case you'd left anyone out.
Norman Good God. What do you take me for?
Ruth I took you for a husband, Norman. Very foolishly. I can feel my
   life expectancy shortening minute by minute. After this week-end, it's
   down by five years.
Norman Don't blame me. I haven't done anything.
Ruth What?
Norman Tom's happy. He's forgiven me.
Ruth Tom is an idiot.
Norman He's a shrewd man. He realized it wasn't serious, Annie and me.
   Just a mad idea. We were both depressed. I wanted to cheer her up,
   that's all.
Ruth Well, next time, send her a funny postcard.
Norman There won't be a next time. I'm concentrating on you.
Ruth Oh, God.
Norman I'll be sorry to leave. I like it down here. Must have been nice
   to grow up in this house. Was it nice?
Ruth All right. I'd nothing against the house. It was the people I didn't
   care for.
Norman You don't know when you're well off. When I think of my
   childhood, the little pokey back-to-back terrace . . .
Ruth Overlooking Regent's Park
Norman Hyde Park.
Ruth Well . . .
Norman The unfashionable side. The slums of South Kensington. They
   were hard days, lass. Anyway, Hyde Park's not country. It's just an
   underground car park with a grass roof. Shall we have a party tonight?
Ruth No, we won't.
Norman Go on. That'd be fun.
Ruth I'm much too tired.

Norman Right. We'll go to bed. We'll go to bed.
Ruth I said I'm tired.
Norman To rest. We'll rest.
Ruth I know you and your rests. Your mind just doesn't associate beds with sleep at all. I don't know when you do sleep. It certainly isn't with me.
Norman I was brought up to believe it was very insulting to sleep with your wife or any lady. A gentleman stays eagerly awake on one elbow. He sleeps at his work. That's what work's for. Why do you think they have the SILENCE notices in the library? So as not to disturb me in my little nook behind the biography shelves. L–P.
Ruth They'll sack you.
Norman They daren't. I reorganized the Main Index. When I die the secret dies with me. (*He "dies"*)

Tom enters from the tennis court

Tom Well, that's done it.
Norman Done what?
Tom The thing on your car. I've fixed it back on.
Norman I thought we needed wire.
Tom No. It screwed on. Don't need wire.
Norman This vet is a genius.
Tom No. The same thing happened on mine. They're always falling off, those things.
Norman Brilliant.
Ruth Do you think someone should tell Reg? He's still hunting for wire, you know.
Tom Oh, good Lord, is he? I'd better tell him.
Norman No. Let me . . .
Tom It's all right, I'll . . .
Norman Please. Let me. I want to see his face. (*Calling*) Reg . . .

Norman goes off gleefully into the house

Ruth He's so bouncy this morning, I could kick him.
Tom Yes. Well—er . . .
Ruth Oh, do stop looking like that, Tom.
Tom What?
Ruth Embarrassed and furtive.
Tom Well, I was just . . . (*He sits*)
Ruth Forget all about it. It was a misunderstanding.
Tom I don't usually grab hold of women in that way, you know.
Ruth I do realize.
Tom I don't want you to get the impression I . . .
Ruth I haven't.
Tom As long as you appreciate . . . (*He pauses*)
Ruth It's a pity you don't, in a way.

Tom What?

Ruth Grab hold a bit more.

Tom How do you mean?

Ruth Annie, for instance. She might even appreciate it.

Tom Oh, I don't think so. I don't think she goes in for that sort of thing.

Ruth Apart from with Norman.

Tom Ah. (*A pause*) That's a good point. Hadn't looked at it quite like that.

Ruth I think you should.

Tom Women are really dreadfully complicated, aren't they? Or do I mean human beings?

Ruth They can be one and the same.

Tom I mean, with other animals, well the majority of them, they're either off heat or on heat. Everyone knows where they are. I probably should have been born a horse or something. With Annie, I never really know. I mean, just now I was chatting away with her about something or other—she started breaking a plate.

Ruth What?

Tom Smashing a plate. No reason. Just simply smashing a plate. I hardly like to say anything to her, when she's like that. In case she starts on me.

Ruth I think she might, shortly.

Reg comes out angrily. Norman follows, gleeful

Tom rises

Reg (*to Tom*) Well, thank you very much.

Tom All right.

Reg You might have told me it screwed. I've wasted half an hour looking for fuse wire that isn't where it should be.

Tom Sorry. I thought you knew it screwed.

Reg If I'd known it screwed, I wouldn't—and this herbert isn't much help, sniggering away.

Ruth Norman, stop sniggering.

Norman I am not sniggering. These are joyful guffaws.

Reg Did you put the top on again?

Tom No. I thought you might want to . . .

Reg Right. Norman.

Norman What?

Reg Come and do something useful for once.

Norman If it's only for once.

Reg We'll put it together. I'll tow you as far as the top of the hill and then you can roll her down, Ruth. That should start her. Oh. One moment. Have I got my tow rope. I don't think I have. I think I took it out to make room for the cases. Do you carry a tow rope?

Norman No idea. We've lost the key of the boot.

Reg How do you open it?

Ruth We haven't. For months.
Reg Oh, grief . . .

Annie comes out

Norman My gym shoes are in there, too.
Reg Annie.
Norman And my football.
Annie Hallo.
Norman Never mind, it will rust away eventually.
Reg Annie, have we got such a thing as a rope? Big thick one.
Annie I think there's one in the cellar. It's very heavy.
Reg Just the job. Tom.
Tom Um?
Reg You fetch the rope.
Tom Rope?
Annie It's in the cellar. Foot of the steps.
Tom Oh. Right. Rope.

Tom goes into the house

Reg Norman, follow me.

Reg strides off through the tennis court

Norman (*following Reg*) Must be marvellous to be a leader of men.

Norman goes off through the tennis court

Ruth I think we're going to spend another night here at this rate.
Annie Oh well, it's no bother.
Ruth I think it's better if we don't. This country air has a disastrous
    effect on some of us. Not that I blame anyone particularly. Least of all
    you. Looking after that woman's enough to turn you completely.
Annie I'm sorry. I've said I'm sorry.
Ruth Why should you be? It was entirely Norman's fault.
Annie Not really. I was feeling lonely and sorry for myself . . .
Ruth Yes, I'm sure you were. That doesn't excuse Norman.
Annie He was lonely, too.
Ruth Norman? Nonsense. What's Norman got to be lonely about? Sorry
    for himself may be. No, he just can't bear not to be the centre of attention.
    Anyway, we won't talk about Norman. He gets talked about enough.
    Which is why he does these things in the first place. You and Tom . . .
Annie Yes.
Ruth Do try and sort out something between you, will you? You can't
    let it drag on and on. It's really absurd. You both want to get together,
    you both should. Look, it's a lovely day. As soon as we've all gone, sit
    Tom down out here and tell him point-blank, either he marries you or

comes and lives with you, or whatever it is you both want, or else he clears off for good. That'll do it. Be so much more convenient. And then we wouldn't have to worry about you.

Annie Which would also be convenient.

Ruth Well, we do worry and there's no point in you giving up everything for Mother's sake. You'll turn into a martyr like Sarah which would be too dreadful for words. Two of you in the family.

Annie Don't worry.

Ruth You can't sit around smashing crockery for the rest of your life. It's sometimes quite satisfying but it's no substitute for the real thing.

Annie Who told you about that?

Ruth Tom.

Annie Oh.

Ruth Who else?

Annie No-one.

Sarah comes out, holding some fuse wire

Sarah There. Fuse wire. It wasn't where he said at all. I knew it wasn't. He wouldn't believe me till he'd seen for himself. Do you know where I found it?

Annie In the pantry on the second shelf.

Sarah Fancy keeping it in the pantry. Who on earth keeps fuse wire in a pantry?

Annie People who have fuse boxes in their pantry.

Sarah Look at the time. Where is he then? I'd better give this to him.

Ruth I wouldn't bother.

Sarah Why?

Ruth He doesn't need it.

Sarah Doesn't need it? What do you mean, he doesn't need it?

Reg enters

Reg Now then.

Sarah What do you mean you don't need it?

Reg Need what?

Sarah This fuse wire you've been going on about.

Reg Oh, we fixed that hours ago.

Sarah Do you realize that I have been . . .

Reg We couldn't wait all day for you, could we? Right. We're ready to go.

Annie What about your rope?

Reg Ah. I had it. Had it all the time. Thought I'd taken it out but I hadn't.

Norman enters

Norman All knots secured, skipper.

Ruth Has he tied the tow rope?

Reg Yes.
Ruth Check it.
Norman What do you mean? We old nautical men. I'll have you know
I've crossed the Serpentine in my day. Couldn't do it now, blast it.
(*He sits*) Not with this old peg leg.
Ruth Come on, Norman.

Norman gets up

Reg I'll tow you as far as the top of the hill, right? We'll disconnect the
rope and then you're free to roll her down. But for heaven's sake wait
till I'm out of the way.
Norman This could be fun.
Sarah Come along, we're very late. (*Giving Annie the fuse wire*) Good-bye,
Annie. Thank you for—looking after us . . .
Annie You're welcome.
Reg See you at Christmas. If not before.
Sarah I shouldn't think before.
Reg No, no. Well . . .
Ruth 'Bye 'bye, Annie.
Annie 'Bye.
Norman Take care.
Annie Yes.
Sarah 'Bye.

All except Annie start to leave

Reg (*as they go*) Now keep your hand brake on till I give you the word.
I don't want you rolling into the back of me.
Ruth All right, all right . . .

They go

Annie watches them out of sight. She turns back to the house

Norman darts on again

Norman (*an urgent whisper*) Annie! Annie!
Annie Norman. What are you . . .
Norman Just came to say good-bye.
Annie Oh, Norman, you're . . .
Norman I'll give you a ring. Can I?
Annie Yes, if you . . .
Norman Next time I'll plan it a bit better, Annie. I promise I'll fix it well
in advance—so that . . .
Annie Norman . . .
Norman What?
Annie We can't.
Norman Of course we can. You'd like to, wouldn't you? Wouldn't you?
Annie Yes, but . . .

Norman I'll fix it. Don't worry.
Annie You said that last time. Look what happened. We upset everybody.
Ruth, Tom, Sarah.
Norman We love each other, don't we?
Annie (*wearily*) I don't know.

A car horn sounds. Norman dashes behind the statue, then reappears

Norman You'd be happy with me, wouldn't you? You'd be happy.
Annie Yes.
Norman (*moving to embrace her*) Oh, Annie—oh God. (*He is entangled in the brambles*) These damn things again.
Annie All right. Keep still. (*Clearing the brambles*) Keep still.
Norman Oh, Annie—ow!
Annie There we are.

The car horn sounds again

Norman I don't want to lose you, Annie.
Annie They're waiting.
Norman I won't lose you, will I, Annie?
Annie Not if you don't want to . . .
Norman I don't. I really don't.

Two car horns sound in unison

Annie Go on, Norman, go on.
Norman Good-bye, I love you. Good-bye.

Norman goes off through the tennis-court, blowing kisses back to her

Annie Oh, Norman . . . (*She stands for a second*)

Tom comes out from the house laden with a very heavy coil of rope

Tom Here we are. Is this the one? (*Looking round*) Oh. Where are they?
Annie They've gone.
Tom They'll need this.
Annie They've got one.
Tom Oh. Wasted journey.
Annie Yes.
Tom Oh well . . . (*He stands, the rope still on his shoulder, where it remains throughout the scene*) Peace and quiet again, eh?
Annie Yes.
Tom Quite a week-end. (*She sits*)
Annie Yes.
Tom I must say, I'm rather relieved Ruth's gone. After my incident. Bit embarrassing.
Annie Yes.
Tom Expect you're glad to see the back of Norman, aren't you? For the same reason. Yes. You must be. (*Pause*) Look. Annie . . .

Annie Mmm?

Tom (*sitting in the other chair*) I've been piecing things together in my mind—fitting the various bits to fill in the picture—building a sort of overall view of things—so I can more or less get an objective angle on it and—er—well, I expect you know what I'm going to say next?

Annie Honestly, Tom, I couldn't begin to guess.

Tom Oh. Was rather hoping you might. Make it all a bit—save me a— it's a shame we're not horses.

Annie What are you talking about, Tom?

Tom Well. It seems to me—that we ought to find a way of—well sorting out our relationship—if we have one—to such a degree that we—come together more or less on a permanent basis. Temporarily at least.

Annie Are you talking about marriage?

Tom Yes.

Annie Oh.

Tom And no.

Annie Which is it?

Tom Well, it could be a lot looser . . .

Annie As loose as we are now, you mean?

Tom No. I meant a bit tighter than that. Somewhere in between. Well, loose and tight. The whole hog if you want to. It's up to you.

Annie I see.

Tom What do you say?

A silence

Annie . . .

A silence

Would you like me to marry you? I would. Like me to marry you. May I? I want to.

Annie (*at length*) I don't know.

Tom Oh.

Annie I'll see.

Tom Oh. I got the idea that perhaps that's what you would have liked.

Annie I did, I think. I'm sorry, Tom, you'll have to wait.

Tom How long for?

Annie At least until I've had a chance to—go away somewhere. And think about it.

Tom Oh, I see. Fair enough.

Pause

Tom Going to be a scorcher today, again.

Annie Yes.

Tom Far too nice to do any work. It's on days like this you really feel at peace with the world. That's what I feel . . .

Two loud horns sound, followed by a distant crash of colliding vehicles. Annie and Tom jump up

(*Recovering*) Good grief.

Annie It's them.

Tom Hang on. Stay there. Stay there—this could be nasty.

Annie Quickly, we must . . . (*She starts to move away*)

Tom (*pushing her back*) No, please, Annie—stay there. Stay there.

Tom rushes off through the tennis court

Annie stands anxiously. Loud shouts are heard off

Reg (*off*) You bloody fool.

Reg stamps on followed by Ruth and Sarah. Sarah is flustered. Norman follows up the rear with Tom

Reg What the hell did you let him drive for?

Ruth He insisted.

Tom Everyone all right?

Reg Why him? Why him?

Sarah I feel terribly faint.

Norman You can't expect Ruth to drive.

Reg Why not?

Norman She hasn't got her glasses.

Reg She could drive better than you blindfolded. Where were your brakes?

Tom Any casualties?

Sarah I feel giddy.

Reg I told you distinctly. Wait till I'm out of the way.

Norman My mistake.

Reg Your mistake? You weren't even in gear.

Sarah I need a glass of water.

Tom I'm not a doctor but I am a vet. If anyone needs any treatment.

Annie Is there much damage?

Norman Yes . . .

Ruth hits Norman with his woolly hat, then throws it on the ground. He sits on the barrel.

We smashed his whole back end in.

Reg I know you've smashed the whole back end in. The damn cars are twisted together like bloody spaghetti.

Annie sits Reg down in a chair

Sarah I've never been so shaken.

Ruth Sit down, Sarah.

Sarah sits

Annie Do you want to phone? Phone the AA?

Reg Some people have as much sense as a—you won't get home today, you know that?

Sarah Well, we'll stay, dear, we'll stay.

Reg I'll have to phone home as well. (*Rising*) Somebody get the cases out? I'll do the phoning. (*To Ruth*) Why did you let him drive? You know what he's like? You knew he was Norman, didn't you?

Reg goes indoors

Norman My mistake.

Tom I'll start fetching the cases, shall I?

Sarah Thank you, Tom. I'm so shaky, I . . .

Tom You stay there.

Sarah I will.

Tom Everyone stay there. Reg and I have got it under control.

Tom goes off through the tennis-court. Ruth sits

Norman (*rising*) Definitely my mistake . . . (*He picks up his hat*)

A silence. Norman stands regarding the three women. They look at him

Norman Well. Back again.

Annie Oh, Norman . . . (*She sits on the barrel*)

Ruth If I didn't know you better, I'd say you did all that deliberately.

Norman Me? Why should I want to do that?

Sarah Huh.

Norman Give me one good reason why I'd do a thing like that?

Ruth Offhand, I can think of three.

Pause

Norman Ah. (*Brightening*) Well, since we're all here, we ought to make the most of it, eh? What do you say?

Norman smiles round at the women in turn

Ruth gets up and without another word goes into the house

(*After her*) **Ruth** . . .

He turns to Annie but she too, rises and goes into the house

Annie . . .

He turns to Sarah. She, likewise, rises and follows the others

Sarah!

Norman is left alone, bewildered, then genuinely hurt and indignant

(*Shouting after them*) I only wanted to make you happy.

CURTAIN

FURNITURE AND PROPERTY LIST

ACT I

Scene 1

On stage: Garden bench
Wheelbarrow
Half a barrel upturned with empty cup and saucer on it
Statue with brambles over it and trailing
In house:
2 easy chairs
2 cushions on window-seat
Bookcase with lamp on top

Round table with plant

Off stage: Gardening gloves, scissors, 6 roses (**Annie**)
Small battered suitcase with pair of pyjamas in cellophane (**Norman**)
2 suitcases (**Reg**)
Bundle of magazines tied with string (**Reg**)

Personal: **Reg:** bag with 1 toffee
Sarah: handbag
Wrist watch for **Reg, Sarah, Tom, Annie**

Scene 2

Off stage: Salad basket (**Reg**)
Apron (**Reg**)
Bottle of home-made parsnip wine and 2 glasses (**Annie**)
Pillow-case (**Annie**)

ACT II

Scene 1

Set: 2 folding garden chairs leaning against barrel
Ruth's handbag on terrace, down stage end

Off stage: Insecticide spray (**Sarah**)
Tennis ball (**Reg**)
Tray (**Sarah**)

Scene 2

Off stage: "Grease" for **Reg's** hands
Rag (**Reg**)
Roll of gardening wire (**Sarah**)
Fuse wire (**Sarah**)
Large coil of rope (**Tom**)

Personal: **Ruth:** handbag, watch

LIGHTING PLOT

Property fittings required: exterior lamp, table lamp
Exterior. A garden. The same scene throughout

ACT I, SCENE 1. Evening

To open: Effect of early evening summer sunshine

No cues

ACT I, SCENE 2. Late evening

To open: Patchy light through trees. Exterior lamp on
           Table lamp on

No cues

ACT II, SCENE 1. Morning

To open: Effect of bright sunshine

No cues

ACT II, SCENE 2. Morning

To open: As Scene 1

No cues

EFFECTS PLOT

ACT I

SCENE 1

Cue 1   **As CURTAIN rises**   **(Page 1)**
Bird song: continue for a few moments, then fade

SCENE 2

No cues

ACT II

SCENE 1

Cue 2   **As CURTAIN rises**   **(Page 25)**
Bird song as before

SCENE 2

Cue 3   **As CURTAIN rises**   **(Page 37)**
Bird song as before

Cue 4   **Annie: "I don't know."**   **(Page 46)**
Car horn

Cue 5   **Annie: "There we are."**   **(Page 46)**
Car horn

Cue 6   **Norman: "I really don't."**   **(Page 46)**
Two car horns together, impatient

Cue 7   **Tom: "That's what I feel. . ."**   **(Page 47)**
2 loud car horns, followed by a crash of colliding vehicles

MADE AND PRINTED IN GREAT BRITAIN BY
LATIMER TREND & COMPANY LTD PLYMOUTH

MADE IN ENGLAND